W9-ATQ-370

THE TWISTED IMAGE

BY ARTHUR GOODFRIEND

If You Were Born in Russia
The Only War We Seek
What Can a Man Believe?
What Can a Man Do?
Something Is Missing . . .
What Is America?
Rice Roots
Stand Fast in Liberty

United States Government Publications

When the Communists Came
Two Sides of One World
Paths of Action toward Asian-American Understanding and Cooperation
Indonesia: A Case Study in Asian-American Understanding

THE

NEW YORK | ST MARTIN'S PRESS

E
188.8
.I4
G6

TWISTED IMAGE

Arthur Goodfriend

115699

Copyright © Arthur Goodfriend 1963
All rights reserved
Library of Congress Catalog Card Number: 63–9426
Manufactured in the United States of America
by H. Wolff, New York

To Francis Patrick Corrigan, Junior,
of the United States Information Service,
who died in the line of duty in
Luang Prabang, Laos, March 31, 1961

12/6/61 JOS. O'GARA 3.00

Foreword

The Vice President of the United States returned from his first visit to Asia troubled by "America's failure to put across to millions of people overseas its desires and real objectives."

"It is a sad but true fact," said Lyndon Johnson, "that our Communist adversaries have been able to convince many that humanitarian projects like Point IV are instruments of imperialism, the simplest moves to defend ourselves are moves of aggression, and honest and openhearted efforts to secure arms control are merely intended to obscure issues."

Echoing the often-voiced lament that "a nation that knows how to popularize commodities ranging all the way from cornflakes to luxury automobiles should be able to tell the rest of the world the simple truth about what it is doing and why it is doing it," the Vice President called for "a straightforward analysis of the reasons for our failure to communicate to the rest of the world."

This book deals with our failure. It chronicles one American's efforts to achieve understanding of another culture, and to bring to others some appreciation of his own.

The focus is India, not yet awakened to reality by Red China's attack: a showcase of the difficulties we face in communicating with Asians, Africans, and others undergoing revolutionary change.

The action occurs within the United States Information Agency, charged by the President and Congress with responsibility for promoting better understanding of the United States among the peoples of the world.

It is not the purpose of this book to cast discredit on any agency or individual in government. On the contrary, the writer values the propaganda function, and respects the dedicated men and women who wrestle daily with the intricacies of the human heart and mind. In the United States Information Agency, certainly, both wisdom and skill abound. Its errors—if errors they are—are honest.

The intent, rather, is to share with the public a dilemma more complex than any single individual or agency, however gifted, can solve alone. Dealing with mankind's understanding, the task invokes the understanding of the American people. It is a problem only they, in their own genius and through their own actions, can dispose.

This book is written in the hope that its message may have meaning to all concerned with America's twisted image, and with freedom's response to the totalitarian challenge.

A.G.

Washington, D.C.

Contents

Let it be clear that this Administration recognizes the value of daring and dissent—that we greet healthy controversy as the hallmark of healthy change.

JOHN F. KENNEDY

We must see to it that the public knows the facts. It must have more information than its own governments are willing to make available.

DEAN RUSK

The Voice of America mirrors this land to the rest of man. It expresses the belief that the common denominator of mankind is surely man himself.

EDWARD R. MURROW

THE TWISTED IMAGE

I. The mental reservation

Two blocks west of the White House stood the headquarters of the United States Information Agency. A
plaque on the cornerstone advertised its mission: "Telling
America's story to the world." A short walk on the ninth
floor brought me to the office of Vincent Patton, Chief of
Operations for Central Asia. The anteroom contained a
battered desk, an overstuffed leather couch, a bookcase
half filled with gray paperbacked reports of congressional
hearings—a shabby inheritance from administrations long
bygone. The only contemporary notes were struck by a
pin-pocked map of Asia and an airline's calendar marking
the date, December 1, 1957.

A balding, keen-eyed man, Patton shook my hand
warmly. He said I was scheduled for a few weeks of orientation on Agency operations. He advised that I plan to
take off for my post—New Delhi, India—as soon as the
course was completed. Then, my right hand raised, I was
sworn into the Foreign Service.

As I took the oath, I sensed something akin to a mental reservation. It was not that I flinched at the prospect of becoming a propagandist. For almost a year my family and myself had lived in an Indonesian village, studying the life cycle of an Asian people. We had learned, at the rice roots, the subleties of the Communist conspiracy. Its capabilities in countries where people were poor in everything but pride and the determination to prosper had become vividly clear. Equally vivid were the blemishes on the American image, both the smears of the Communists and those inflicted by our own exports of lurid literature and films. The need to cleanse our reputation, to make common cause with other peoples, to open effective exchanges of information and ideas between Asians and ourselves was compelling. Whatever connotation propaganda might have in other minds, in mine it was invested with honor and urgency.

My reservation centered on the Information Agency itself. Despite the importance of its function, it remained an object of widespread cynicism and disapproval. Notwithstanding the advice of citizens' advisory commissions drawn from advertising, publishing, public relations, communications, the behavioral sciences—controversy clouded the Agency's activities. Agency outposts around the world were called the United States Information Service (USIS). From these came massive evidence of American effectiveness in propaganda. Such evidence did little to dispel doubt about USIA and USIS operations. Though proofs multiplied of Soviet and Chinese incursions into everdeeper realms of human reason and emotion, the Agency was still derided. James Reston summed up the national frustration in *The New York Times:* "No country ever had a better story to tell or failed so lamentably to tell it well. . . ."

Each year, led by the Director, Agency officials climbed the Hill to plead their case before Congress and returned withered by criticism. Months of preparation by the Agency's top talent, salvos of statistics, echoes of communism's intensifying cannonade—nothing seemed capable of convincing Congress that the dollars USIA spent on propaganda did much good. On the contrary, as one Senator put it: "The more money we spend, the worse off we get."

Senators were baffled by the intangibility of the Agency's output. Voice of America broadcasts vanished into air. Words printed in bizarre languages offered little evidence of being read. Sooner or later, some Senator was certain to say, "Let's be realistic about this. There is more and more hostility toward the United States. These information programs are not paying off." Or, "Now let us get to the fundamental thing. I want to know what effect we are achieving. That is what constantly bothers me." It was a difficult question to answer. When Agency officials tried, they frequently found themselves either making exaggerated claims or taking credit for successes in which the Agency's role was minimal.

In disparagement of the Agency, members of the House were even less restrained than the Senate. Their qualms covered a wide gamut, from audiences reached per dollar expended in Burma to "giveaways" of encyclopaedias in Laos. Be it expenses for transportation or moneys allotted for entertainment—known on the Hill as "the booze allowance"—every penny was scrutinized with a ferocity that gave the most stalwart Agency officials the jitters.

The Agency's bugbear was the Congressman from New York, John J. Rooney, chairman of the House subcommittee that passed on USIA budget requests. Brilliant, remorseless, indefatigable, he left witnesses in little doubt about how cheaply he valued their words, how dearly he counted the dollars they expended. Like a sidewinder missile, he swooped toward his target whenever a witness showed signs of warmth around the collar. Time and again he shattered a nervous officer with a burst of irony, making a shambles of his months of earnest effort.

The record of the Agency's duel with Representative Rooney made dismal reading. In hearing after hearing, the dialogue was repeated. A typical interchange occurred at the time I entered the Agency.

"What is the film," Chairman Rooney asked the Chief of the Agency's Motion Picture Service, "to which you would refer as your most successful production?"

"That is a difficult question to answer," the Chief replied, "because frankly, I think most of them have been successful. However, if I had to pick one picture that has made the most impact of any film that has been produced, I would certainly have to say the 'Hungarian Fight for Freedom' has had the most effect on the world audience."

The Chairman: "Something happened spontaneously that you had nothing to do with, and you point to that as your best film?"

The Chief: "I would say we had a good deal to do with the film. Obviously we had nothing to do with the events that we were able to show in the film, but the ability to take advantage of a dramatic illustration of the total failure of the Communist system, there is no way that I can see that anything is quite so dramatic."

The Chairman: "Assuming that is your four-star film, what would you say is your three-star film?"

The Chief: "Mr. Chairman, you are asking me like a father to choose among his children. It is a very difficult question."

The Chairman: "I would assume from that remark that you have no films this year that are better than the ones you showed us last year and the year before?"

The Chief: "I hoped that the films we showed you last year were impressive."

The Chairman: "As far as I am concerned, they were not impressive. I have not yet met that Member that thought they were impressive. . . . This is the only body of the two Houses which looked at these films. We were most amazed that you thought we approved the films produced by you. The fact of the matter is that we always have been highly critical of them."

In another significant exchange, Representative Rooney inserted into the record the observations of a man described as "a quite substantial American citizen, a member of the legal profession, who spent some time in certain South American countries." According to this unidentified source:

Our propaganda does not reach the average citizen. It gives the impression of being directed toward the prosperous, satisfied upper class. We don't seem to realize that a new middle class is developing, and that the laboring class is beginning to take an interest in politics and the betterment of its economic conditions. In content, our propaganda does not concentrate on the actual problems facing the average citizen. We frequently write over the head, or at least, over the interest, of the average man. Emphasis on our higher standards of living and our material possessions frequently causes resentment rather than a desire to emulate us. Poor propaganda is sometimes worse than none at all.

The Agency responded to these charges in a formal statement.

We do not address ourselves to general or undifferentiated audiences. We do not have the capacity for reaching directly the large mass of people in the area. But we aim for and do reach selected individuals and groups. In each country we determine which groups and which individuals are the most important, either because of their strength within the country, or their capacity to influence public opinion in their own right. For example, in a country where the comparatively small intellectual and student classes are the key elements in the population, a major USIS task may be to convince these groups that the United States has achieved a high level of intellectual maturity, as evidence of capacity for international leadership. A conscious effort is made, therefore, to produce a scholarly output designed to interest and influence these intellectual opinion moulders.

The dialogue, as ever, was indecisive. Congress thrust. The Agency parried. Inadequacies were charged but rarely proved. A defense was entered, but rarely clinched. Whatever was wrong with the USIA, it was a hardy perennial. Neither annual budget hearings nor special investigations could isolate or eradicate the virus. Senator Joseph McCarthy blamed the Agency's troubles on Communist infiltration. In his efforts to exorcise Communists, he almost immolated the Agency. A Senate Foreign Relations Committee under Bourke Hickenlooper concluded that the psychological strategy of the United States was in bad shape. It asked that the President deal with the problem as "a matter of urgency." In the gross spectacle of Congress-Agency discord, the Agency's reputation was not enhanced. An impression gained ground that where there was so much smoke, there must be fire.

The nation's press was hardly more enthusiastic than the Congress. In a poll of fifty-five foreign correspondents in forty-one countries, some correspondents opined that "USIS is doing a competent job." Others submitted that "somehow the conclusion is inescapable that our propaganda program has gotten off on the wrong track and needs to be started all over again." Reporters agreed that "a repeated recital of the advantages of America as a place to live excites more envy than admiration." Boastfulness and high pressure were decried. USIS officers were urged to mingle more with the masses. "Too much time is spent in air-conditioned offices in the larger cities and not enough perspiring alongside the people." Rating USIS personnel, on the whole, as "earnest, hard working, adequate," the foreign correspondents nevertheless chided USIS "as a machine that lacks imagination and flexibility," operated by "routine people," "unimaginative bureaucrats," and "do-gooders."

In general, the nation's newspapers accorded little space to the Agency's operations. This pattern changed only when an old director was dismissed and a new director was appointed by the President. Then, always, a rash of editorials erupted across the land. Rarely rating the new incumbent as less than a first-class choice, editorial writers and columnists wished him success in the "difficult job of selling America abroad." Coupled with this implied respect for the activity, inevitably, was a note of chagrin at its failure to date. Again and again, one heard the same refrain: "The United States has spent more time and energy learning the arts of persuasion than all the countries of the world put together. . . . Yet our propaganda has been a spectacular flop from beginning to end."

The separation of foreign policy-making and propaganda was singled out by some as the heart of the problem. "It seems," in one journalist's words, "as if policy is first elaborated and then tossed to the propaganda boys to make the best of it, whereas they ought to have been in at the birth." Walter Lippmann, for one, opposed this view. In the process, he expressed the antagonism to propaganda that underlay the Agency's difficulties:

The Secretary of State cannot afford to be regarded as a propagandist. To be an effective Secretary of State he must have the confidence of the Foreign Ministers and the Prime Ministers with whom he negotiates. He must be known as a man of his word, as one who uses words precisely which mean genuinely what they say. Now there is no use pretending that this is the moral standard in psychological warfare. Words are used by the propagandist not to convey the whole truth as he knows it but to work an effect on other men's minds—to sell them a notion and to "engineer their consent."

"That is why," Mr. Lippmann concluded, "the Secretary of State and the foreign service should remain aloof and uncontaminated by propaganda."

American businessmen operating in foreign markets showed a similar lack of enthusiasm about the Agency. Four hundred overseas representatives of companies were polled by the United States Chamber of Commerce. About half the replies constituted an endorsement of the Agency's mission, personnel, and performance. The other half was hesitant. Many businessmen shared the feeling that "our information program is disseminated among neo-intellectuals, upper levels, the social elite, and others who are already on our side, and need little or no convincing. On the other hand, the Communist effort is directed at the laboring classes, students, underprivileged or underpaid groups, the country's younger actual and potential leaders. It has more general effect than ours." The Chamber of Commerce report concluded that "our propaganda effort can be improved."

As for the general public, letters to editors beat with indignation at America's inability to articulate its message. Some urged an uncompromising assertion of United States power to stiffen our friends and frighten our foes. Others favored an all-out anti-Communist campaign to educate the world to its peril. Another segment of opinion disagreed, favoring an approach eloquently expressed by Henri Peyre, head of Yale University's French Department, in a letter to *The New York Times*.

Is it not possible for our propaganda abroad to show what our ideals are, in spheres other than technological? Can we not stress the way we live our religion? Can we not describe the gigantic progress of science and of medicine in America over the last forty years, not in the spirit of childish boastfulness, but stressing our devotion to supranational ideals? India, the Middle East, the Muslim world need and want some share of material comfort, but not at the price of their spiritual ideals. Can we not answer the anguished appeal of these nations? Democracy is a much abused and distrusted word in many lands today; but freedom, generosity, trust in one's fellow being, fraternity, still are potent words, and they are virtues which this country honors. Instead of the childish saber-rattling which even Khrushchev condemned recently, and the swaggers over the gadgetry of comfort, America could appear abroad as eager for peace and cooperation, confident in the values of the spirit, ready to help other people be themselves and not copyists of the American technology if it does not suit them.

Flatly contradicting all this criticism was the Agency's self-appraisal of its own performances. Its semiannual *Review* contained accounts of substantial accomplishment in every area of the world. The issue circulating around Washington in December, 1957, contained thirty-eight pages of "highlights." These revealed that the opportunities afforded by the Hungarian revolt had been fully exploited by a documentary film, press reports, a photographic exhibit and around-the-clock news coverage by the Voice of America. The Suez Crisis had been met with a strong step-up in VOA Arabic broadcasts, and by circulating texts of statements by the President and other United States officials. An information officer in Iraq was quoted: "Almost no paper in Baghdad went to press without a last-minute call to USIS to get latest developments." In Bombay, an editor was reported as "killing an anti-American story after seeing an actual Eisenhower text excluding the use of force in Suez."

The graver the situation in a given area, the brighter the USIS tidings. *America Illustrated*, the Agency's Russian language magazine, was reported as "a best seller in the Soviet Union." A film on President Sukarno's visit to the United States was described as "playing to standing room only audiences in Indonesia." An exhibit featuring Eisenhower's "Open Skies for Peace" proposal was winning kudos wherever it was shown. America's cultural story was being told by art displays, English classes, and performing artists covering every continent. These, it appeared, were overcoming foreign prejudice against the cultural sterility and materialism of American civilization. As though to banish any doubt, the Voice of America's symposium on Frontiers of Knowledge broadcast the views of the world's leading thinkers on subjects ranging from religion to outer space.

Together with earlier issues, the *Review* provided an insight into the Agency's self-image. With annual budgets touching $130 million—about as much as one American corporation spends to advertise soap—the scope of the Agency's global responsibility dwarfed the dollars expended. The Communists' outlays were conservatively estimated at about six times the Agency's. To jam the free world's broadcasts alone, the Soviet Bloc was said to be spending more than the United States invested in the entire Information Agency.

Altogether, the Agency consisted of 10,700 employees: 2,500 Americans at home, 1,200 Americans overseas, and 7,000 nationals of other countries employed by USIS posts. There were 185 of these posts in 85 countries. Output was enormous. The Voice of America broadcast more words per day than CBS and NBC combined. It reached from forty to fifty million people per day in thirty-seven languages. The Agency's press service supplied USIS posts with 40,000 words a day, plus thousands of photos. Seventy-eight periodicals were published for foreign readers. Agency-produced cartoon strips had a larger readership abroad than any commercial strips.

The Television Service was reaching audiences in forty-seven countries. The Agency's Motion Picture Service had either made or acquired over 1200 film titles. Audiences exceeded half a billion people a year. USIA maintained 160 libraries abroad, and contributed to the support of another 105 binational centers—institutions jointly sponsored by American and foreign nationals to provide English language instruction, exhibits, seminars, and other activities conducive to better understanding of America. Hundreds of titles of American books were being translated, published, and sold abroad in inexpensive editions.

Touring American artists were being introduced by USIS to foreign audiences. Through its Office of Private Cooperation, the Agency helped channel the activities of forty separate people-to-people committees toward the realization of American objectives. One of these committees had discovered Van Cliburn and had gotten him over to Moscow to win the Tschaikovsky competition.

The *Review* concluded with a curious vignette. "USIS in Cuba, according to the Havana Post, is doing a real job of winning friends and influencing people. Letters by the sack-load pour in from all parts of the island, testifying to the good work being done."

If the *Review* represented the sophistication and style of an Agency charged with so sensitive a mission, it seemed to me that grave doubts beclouded its fulfillment. The Agency's positive posture was hard to equate with the mysteries that still surrounded the human mind. The unbridled buoyancy, the perfervid house-organ optimism, ill accorded with the somber international situation, so soon to be underscored by events in Cuba and Iraq. The sheer variety and quantity of output gave rise to questions about quality. The crude self-advertisement smacked of disrespect for American intelligence. As for Communist capability, it was ignored, along with any examination of the assumptions underlying the Agency's enormous activity.

I remembered the warning of an old friend who had just left the Agency after almost a decade of service. Upon learning of my decision to join, she minced no words. "Don't!" she urged. "You can't buck the bureaucracy. It will break your heart!"

Of all these things my mental reservation about the United States Information Agency was formed: the critical attitude of Congress, the misgivings of the press, the hesitations of the business community, the puzzlement of the public, the Agency's narcissism, the warning of my friend.

On the other hand, years abroad had made me appreciate the importance of the Agency's role. My hopes for freedom's success, once high, drooped with each day's headlines. Everywhere, it seemed, our dollars had more appeal than our principles. Communist infiltration in Asia, anti-Americanism in Latin America, racism in Africa— none of these augured victory in the crucial struggle of our time.

How were we really faring in the struggle? Was there something fundamentally faulty in our overseas information activity? Or, if the Agency's self-appraisal was correct —if we were indeed scoring successes in every critical area, on every crucial issue—why was America's image so distorted? Why were the Agency's efforts so maligned? On questions such as these, so important to the fate of America, and to the future of human freedom, what were the facts?

Of only one thing was I sure. No consultant studying the Agency on an intermittent basis, no outsider observing its overseas operations an ocean's width away, no congressional investigator with a political ax to grind or a budget to belabor could discern the answers. The one way to understand the Agency and its operation was to join, to serve abroad, to participate in its problems and performance.

We saw Americans as "modern Ben Franklins" mingling with the people. They saw islands of white Western privilege in the ocean of their poverty. We saw America, a God-fearing society with meaning to everyone who prized opportunity, human dignity, freedom. They saw money, materialism, ideals without reality: an America they could not relate to themselves.

The contrast with communism's tactics accented American errors. We had worked exclusively with the existing government; they had infiltrated the unions, schools, barracks, and peoples' organizations. We had concentrated our efforts too long upon the cities; they had gone into the villages. We had tried to win people with charity; they had reached them with political education. We had failed to harness human emotions constructively; they had exploited the human craving for work, joy, and hope.

America could not have saved China. But our failure to see ourselves as others saw us had hardly helped.

In other areas of the world conditions were akin to China's. To profit from our defeat, it seemed to me, we must apply the lessons we had learned too late in China. To win, we must relate our material aid to the spiritual beliefs, the cultural backgrounds, the hopes and woes of other peoples. We must explain our goals and actions in symbols the least literate could understand. We must know and use *their* communications methods. We must make democracy *theirs*, and not ours alone.

Returning to Washington, I put these lessons before the President. Mr. Truman commended them to Dean Acheson, the Secretary of State, and to his newly appointed Assistant Secretary for Public Affairs, Edward W. Barrett. Plucked from the editorial directorship of

Newsweek magazine, Mr. Barrett had quickly come to similar conclusions about America's propaganda. Something affirmative was needed, he felt, to cope with communism's appeal to rising peoples. America's message must speak, not only for America, but for all mankind's hope for peace, prosperity, and freedom. In his words: "The whole overseas information program was not getting down far enough to the people—into the masses where the raw material for communism is so often found. It was not getting out beyond the major cities. It was still too heavily concentrated on the upper crust."

Barrett asked me to return to Asia where the crisis was becoming increasingly acute. My mission was to state America's message in terms of Asian understanding.

I was briefed on what to expect. Overseas, America's information activities centered in the offices of the United States Information Service, familiarly known as USIS. Posts were located in the capitals of each country, with subposts sometimes situated in smaller cities. Each was headed by a Public Affairs Officer, or PAO, responsible to the Assistant Secretary of State. As an adjunct of the American Embassy, however, USIS was also an instrument of the Ambassador, and subject to his will. Some programs, in Barrett's opinion, were excellent. Others were downright bad. They reflected the varying abilities of the PAO's and, to a degree, the public relations propensities of the Ambassadors. What the program lacked was across-the-board professionalism.

My experience had confirmed Ed Barrett's analysis. Our USIS offices were staffed by hard-working men and women, many of whom were imbued with missionary zeal. They enjoyed good relationships with local politicians, university chancellors, press and radio personalities, and attachés of other friendly embassies. They issued press releases and made talks on the American way of life. Assisted by documentary films provided by Washington, they strove to offset Hollywood's gaudy caricature of American modes and manners.

Too weak to be audible in most areas, the Voice of America radio operation was difficult to appraise. Exchange-of-persons programs, however, left little doubt about their desirability. American lecturers, journalists, artists, and entertainers were performing before appreciative audiences. The influence of American teachers on Asian campuses seemed profound. Asian students, after a year's attendance at American universities on Fulbright grants, were returning with enthusiasm for American civilization.

Above all, USIS libraries seemed worth their salt. Nothing surpassed them as mirrors of American thought, and as proof of American access to knowledge. Neither locks, nor glass, nor a disapproving glance discouraged browsers. The simple fact of a book's availability—to barefoot tonga drivers as freely as to Prime Ministers—did more than tracts to teach the meaning of an open society.

On the other hand, Ed Barrett's reservations seemed soundly based. Many USIS officers were simply administrators, journalists, advertising men, or teachers practicing their American professions in a foreign milieu. Few had had any training for the job of communicating with non-Americans. Each followed his own bias or bent. Across Asia, their uneven performance seemed more reflective of individual inspiration than of the inner discipline that marks the professional. Many seemed oblivious to local tastes and taboos; in most posts, knowledge of folkways was almost nil. Above all, amid hunger and despair that numbed the senses, evidence of America's opulence and optimism struck a false note. Nor did recitals of our freedoms appear appropriate among peoples desperate for their daily bread.

Equally disturbing was the city-centered, elite-oriented nature of USIS activity. Some information officers felt bound by the protocol that governed the deportment of their State Department colleagues, wooing the same ministers and magnates at cocktail parties and formal dinners. Diplomatic punctilio often took precedence over the shirt-sleeved, ink-stained, beat-pounding tradition of the communication crafts.

True, many a lock was lubricated, many a gate was opened by judicious infusions of bourbon and branch water into local influentials. The chief disadvantages lay in the utter absorption with Western-educated intellectuals; the barrier interposed between Americans and the miserable commonality; the alcohol-induced euphoria that sometimes obscured unsavory facts. My enjoyment of these parties was impaired by memories of aseptic affairs in Shanghai and Peking in which, except for bearers unctuously serving drinks, the lower classes had no place. However much diplomats might depend on social seduction, communications specialists needed a broader spectrum of contacts to be fully effective.

As matters stood, few USIS personnel had ever worked in the villages, or among the laboring classes in the larger cities. The shadow-play, the song-singer, the storyteller, the soothsayer—the indigenous opinion-molding apparatus through which the Communists were circulating their sinister mixtures of enticement and libel—these were unknown to the average USIS officer, or scorned as too bizarre. Some librarians managed to send books to reading rooms in the out-country where literate villagers might gain some sense of American civilization. But the majority served clienteles drawn from better-class sections of the larger cities.

To break the crust, to thrust beyond, to fuse with the forces of revolutionary change that were transforming Asia: the need seemed as urgent as the peril. But how? To learn the answers, I talked with Asians at every level of life: with farmers, teachers, students, women, workers, village headmen, heads of state. Little by little, from Manila to Karachi, I gained insights into the nature of Asian nationalism—the inner fears behind its advertised ambitions, its respect for tradition, its hunger for modernization, its indigenous arteries of communication, the special relationship between the leaders and the led.

India's political attitudes were typical of southeast Asia. Socialist, suspicious of the West, soft on the Soviet Union and Red China, its leaders clung to the myth that safety lay in nonalignment. At the same time, here reposed those latent Asian strengths that, coupled with the legacy left by Britain, made India a citadel of parliamentary democracy.

In the USIS office in New Delhi, the Public Affairs Officer and I took a hard look at India. Progress was being made in 1951 against great odds. But India remained in danger. Decades must elapse before the people would know a better life. Meanwhile their own government would demand hard work and sacrifice to create the capital needed to generate a modern industrial economy. The Communists, feeding the people's resentments and whipping their impatience, would urge them to quit the tedious democratic path and to leap instead, in one giant Marxist jump, into an age of abundance.

On balance, the outlook was grim. But so, before 1947, had been the prospects of India's independence. All the odds had been against India's ability to endure the long struggle against the British. Whatever it was that had served India so well in the past, sustaining it in the fight for freedom, was doubly needed now in the struggle for national survival. If only we could isolate and understand this potent force, our course of action in India—and Asia —might be clear.

Together, the PAO and I traced the history of India's nationalist movement. Three tendencies were evident throughout. First, a reaffirmation of India's ancient law, Vedanta, cleansed of excrescences that had diminished its vitality. Second, the infusion of Western liberalism into Vedanta, reinvigorating Hinduism and making it the springboard of the nationalist movement. Third, the popularization of the nationalist movement by linking it with the yearnings of the common people.

All the great leaders of India's revolution had been energized by these impulses. The first was the "Father of Modern India," Raja Ram Mohan Roy. An employee of the East India Company in the eighteenth century, he had concluded that only a modernized, reformed, and resurgent Hinduism could end British rule. His movement, called the Society of God, worked to rid Hinduism of idol worship, the hierarchy of castes, child marriage, and other social shackles holding the people in the prison of the past. Infusing India's incipient revolution with the spirit of inquiry sweeping Europe and America, he did not forget to salve Indian ego. Such concepts as the equality of men, the right to self-determination, the legitimacy of self-rule, he claimed, went back to creation and were first voiced by Vedanta.

To purify Hinduism, to forge it into a political weapon, to replace, with a proud self-confidence in Indian tradition, the feelings of abject inferiority implanted by the West—behind these goals Roy's successors strove to mobilize the masses. "Whether the leadership of society lies in the hands of those who monopolize learning, or wield the power of riches or arms, the source of its power is always the subject masses," wrote Swami Vivekananda. "By so much as the class in power severs itself from this source, by so much is it sure to be weak."

Such writers as Benkim Chandra Chatterjee urged fellow intellectuals "to disanglicize ourselves and to speak to the masses in the language which they understand." To give the people pride in their past, Bal Gangadhar Tilak, "Father of Indian Unrest," advocated national festivals honoring the Maratha hero Shivaji and the elephant god, Ganesh. India's revolutionary anthem, "Hail to the Mother," symbolized the peasants' love of the land and their reverence for the female deity. By the evocation of such traditions India's freedom struggle was transformed from an intellectual ideal to a mass movement.

Aurobindo Ghose was yet another of the philosophers who synthesized Vedanta with Jeffersonian democracy. Denouncing the centralized state based on any form of coercion, one of many warnings to the Indian people against totalitarian rule, he turned India's centuries-old faith into a modern weapon of liberation. Coupled with this democratic argument was a plea to the people to be true to themselves, neither dupes nor shadows of predatory powers. "That India," Ghose said, "which must seek now to awake is not an Anglicized Oriental people, docile pupil of the West, and doomed to repeat the cycle of the Occident's success and failure, but still the immovable Shakti—the creative forces of the universe—recovering her deepest self, lifting her head higher toward a supreme source of light and strength, and turning to discover the complete meaning and vaster form of her duty."

In Mohandas Gandhi the Vedic ideal came to full fruition: nonviolent evolution toward independence; economic progress in the village; peace; the exaltation of human dignity, the safeguarding of property; the invocation of the efforts of India's humblest citizens in the achievement of worthy ends through worthy means.

The record showed that India would venerate the understanding teacher. It would welcome assistance in bringing the backward segments of its society into the modern world. But India would not forget the colonial past. It would be sensitive to the slightest hint of Western superiority. India's determination to approach its problems with a strong sense of its own tradition was inflexible. Above all, one warning rang clear. The United States Ambassador to India, Chester Bowles, stated the point succinctly: "The key to Asian peace lies where we have worked for it least: among the people."

America's best course, we agreed, was to follow the grain of Indian experience and idealism. Instead of placing total emphasis on the dissemination of American aims, USIS should identify local aspirations, attempting where possible to harmonize these with our own. Opportunities were infinite. The basis of Hindu and Muslim life was religion. The essence of Hindu and Islamic thought was

God. The family was the keystone of Indian society. Parliamentarian democracy, majority rule, protection of minorities were among the most ancient of Hindu institutions.

For over three thousand years, Indian villages had known self-rule by popularly elected selectmen. The principle of private property, the ownership of land, was sanctioned by Vedic scripture. Much of Hindu literature, art, music, drama, and dance was expressive of individualism. Opposition to atheism, to totalitarianism, to police state practices was as explicit in Indian life as in American.

"What is the universe?" the Upanishads had demanded. "From what does it arise? Into what does it go? And the answer is: In freedom it arises. In freedom it rests. And into freedom it melts away."

The tasks of USIS seemed clear: to fortify India's faith in democracy with local accomplishments as well as with American examples. To define freedom in terms of Indian experience as well as our own, using language and imagery understandable by Indians. To awaken Indians to the dangers communism posed to their most precious values, their territorial integrity, their hard-won independence. At the same time, to rest our case on a positive revelation of democracy's power.

I left Asia in 1951 with no illusions that my mission was accomplished. Assistance to Asia's young nations was insufficient to their need. As long as the gap between awakened wants and fulfillment remained unbridged—as long as Asia's leaders naïvely placed their trust in Moscow's friendship and Peking's pacifism—danger threatened. As for our efforts to relate America's experience and aspirations with Asia's, progress was naturally slow. Oriental cultures were strange. It would take time to gain the true understanding of others which must underlie an effective projection of ourselves. Meanwhile, some USIS officers were unshaken in their conviction that a blunt assertion of the American "position," planted among a handful of "people who count," was the only feasible course of American action. As a result, American policies sometimes seemed tarred with an imperialist brush. Asians were being asked to enlist in a struggle postulated largely in American terms.

But I was not without hope. We had found a way toward the mind of Asia. Under some of our more sensitive Foreign Service officers, American information activities rested on less ethnocentric premises. Asian viewpoints were being considered. We were beginning to talk in a language Asians could understand. Evidence existed that it lay within us to adjust to other ways of life, to establish the inner compatibility of outwardly different folkways, to communicate with other peoples over a bridge of common goals.

Back in Washington, the indigenous approach evolving from the Asian experiment seemed accepted throughout the Information Service. In Ed Barrett's words: "Eager Beavers have learned you don't sell democracy to Danes and Arabs the way you sell soap in Sioux City. Ballyhoo artists must give way to area experts." Less emphasis was placed on simple technical skills and more on knowledge of the customs, tastes, and susceptibilities of overseas audiences. The Service, in short, began to look at Asia through Asian eyes.

So, it seemed, did the new Administration. Shortly after taking office in 1953, President Eisenhower asserted that "the great struggle of our times is one of the spirit. It is a struggle for the hearts and souls of men." To determine how the struggle might be won, he appointed a committee under William H. Jackson to examine America's overseas information program and to make recommendations for its improvement.

Invited to testify before the committee, I said that we had yet to convince other peoples that America honored their heritage and represented their own most cherished values. Most men abided in the shadows of their temples and mosques, and were already committed to Gods and cultures which to them were precious. Given free choice, it seemed reasonable to believe that they would turn to the nation which showed the deepest understanding of their problems and goals, and promised the least violence to their culture. If America seemed too strange, too rich, and too remote, or intent only on selfish aims, we could not earn their trust.

The Jackson committee's report to the President affirmed that the purpose of American propaganda should be "to show the identity of American goals with those of other peoples. These goals and desires which we hold in common must be explained in ways that will cause others to join with us in achieving them."

Responding to the Jackson Committee's recommendations, President Eisenhower split off the information function from the Department of State, and created an independent United States Information Agency. On October 22, 1953, he issued a directive establishing its mission:

The purpose of the United States Information Agency shall be to submit evidence to peoples of other nations by means of communications techniques that the objectives and policies of the United States are in harmony with and will advance their legitimate aspirations for freedom, progress, and peace.

The mandate seemed a long step from the slogans and campaigns of the past. In it I detected the sensitivity in human relationships in which America took pride.

III. Dr. Sharma and Mr. Kapoor

Twenty people pressed into the overheated room. Facing them sat three men. One was middle-aged, light skinned, of medium size, with craggy features, rumpled clothes, a pugnacious air redolent of the Liffey. But the voice bore no trace of a brogue. Its lilting, reedy quality spoke unmistakably of the Ganges. He introduced himself as Dr. Sharma, on a cultural mission from India.

At his side sat a large young man. The jaw of his handsome face was grim; the eyes, beneath brows as thick and black as his curling hair, were cold. "I am," he said in an Oxford accent, "Prem Kapoor."

Facing them was a tall man, spare, with graying hair brushed back from a florid brow. He identified himself as Dave Weed, recently returned to Washington from a USIS post in South America.

"Gentlemen," he said, addressing the two Indians. "I want to welcome you to my country. If you have any questions about our government, our people, our way of life, please feel free to ask. Freedom, you know, is the very lifeblood of America."

Dr. Sharma and Mr. Kapoor looked puzzled. "I beg your pardon," said Dr. Sharma, "but we did not quite understand. What did you say about freedom—and blood?"

Slowly and clearly, Weed repeated. "I said that freedom is the lifeblood of America."

The Indians took a few seconds to ponder Weed's words. When Sharma spoke, his tone dripped venom. "Freedom? Does the Negro have freedom in America? And this lifeblood for which Americans seem so thirsty —is this the Negro lifeblood that flows when he is lynched?"

Weed smiled and shook his head. "I'm afraid you misunderstand. Americans aren't bloodthirsty. All I said is that freedom is in our blood."

"Blood, blood, blood!" Kapoor roared. "Americans think only of blood! First it was the blood of your Indians. Then it was the blood of your Negroes. Then it was Mexican blood, Sacco-Vanzetti blood, Rosenberg blood, Korean blood! Other countries run on coal and oil. Only America runs on blood!"

Weed's pink complexion turned burgundy. Removing a handkerchief from his breast pocket, he dabbed at his brow. "Gentlemen," he said, "let's stick to the point. May I remind you that American Negroes are better off than white men in many parts of the world. They own cars, homes, deep freezes, television sets, insurance policies. They have more money in the bank than nine people out of ten in Latin America, Asia, and Africa have ever seen in their lives."

Sharma snorted. "Bathtubs, telephones, Chevrolets! Americans judge everything in life by gadgets and dollars! No wonder there is so much crime, drunkenness, insanity, divorce! No wonder your capitalist society produces nothing—no music, no art, no ballet!"

"And why," Kapoor interjected, "are Asians and Africans poor? Who made them poor but the imperialist exploiters? It is not good for you to look down on my people because they have no shoes on their feet and no hi-fi in their homes. To them, perhaps, it is more important for workers and peasants to throw out the Yankee money-lenders who suck them dry for interest. Let Wall Street run America. Other countries want to run themselves!"

A quaver in Weed's voice betrayed a fraying temper. "I do not look down on Asians and Africans. On the contrary, our Declaration of Independence specifically states that all men are created equal. That's as true today as when it was written."

Kapoor's lips curled in a sardonic smile. "Am I to understand that all men are created equal because your Declaration of Independence says so? Perhaps they would be created equal without your Declaration. Maybe something can be good without being stamped Made in America!"

Weeds' face was livid. Suddenly he threw up his hands and laughed. "You win," he said. "I know when I'm beaten!"

Sharma and Kapoor smiled, reached over and shook his hand. "Sorry," said Dr. Sharma in a west New York state accent. "We were rougher than usual this morning."

Weed rose. "I sure kept leading with my chin, and you clipped it." He rubbed his jaw ruefully as he left the table and took a seat in the rear of the class.

Mr. Kapoor faced the spectators. "Any comments?" he asked.

Hands went up all over the room.

It was one of the Meet the Critic sessions held by the Training Division of the Information Agency in Washington as part of an eight-week orientation course for persons preparing for service overseas. "Dr. Sharma" was in real life Dr. Paul C. Conroy, a former professor of political science at Canisius College, now a specialist in intercultural communication. "Mr. Prem Kapoor" was Charles Vetter, a Detroit lawyer who during World War II had been handed the job of teaching French cadets to fly American aircraft. Training had gotten into his system. Quitting law, he had teamed up with Conroy in the Agency's Training Division. Together they played innumerable roles as questioning nationals of countries to which trainees would be posted, or as Russians needling Americans with the Marxist-Leninist line. Each of us endured the ordeal of facing them, of having our assumptions upset, our colloquialisms garbled, our facts and figures boomerang and blow up in our faces. When the carnage was complete, the class did a post-mortem on our performances.

Of the eighteen persons in our group, all but four were Junior Officer Trainees, or JOT's: probationers who would have to undergo nine months of exposure to field conditions before being accepted by the Foreign Service. All were college graduates—two had doctorates and five had master's degrees—with practical experience in the newspaper, television, radio, library, or teaching fields.

Of the other four, one, like myself, was a direct entrant into the Foreign Service at a senior grade, by virtue of his professional qualifications. This was Andrew Morelli, a stout man with silver-rimmed spectacles, employed by the Voice of America to manage the facilities at one of its overseas relay stations. The third man was Weed. The fourth was none other than Vince Patton, who only yesterday, as Chief of Operations for Central Asia, had sworn me in!

Behind Patton's presence lay the latest of the misadventures that dogged the Agency. Arthur Larson, USIA's third director under the Eisenhower administration, had recently fallen afoul of Democratic members of Congress for making remarks deemed politically indiscreet in a speech in Honolulu. Rather than expose the Agency to the opprobrium in which he was held on the Hill, he had stepped out. The President had nominated George V. Allen to replace him. For Mr. Allen, veteran of successful ambassadorial tours in India, Yugoslavia, Iran and Greece, it was his second lap around the information arena. No amateur in government, he was shaking up the organization. According to rumor, Vince Patton's demotion from chief of a major area to humble trainee was but the first of other Draconian decisions to come. It was a cruel test of any man. I was not the only one who wondered how Patton would take it.

At first, Vince was given to burying his face in *The Washington Post,* paying scant attention to the instructors or his fellow trainees. Little by little, however, his interest had been engaged by Conroy and Vetter; he was soon an avid listener and taker of notes. At lunch one day he told me why.

"The Agency is full of serious officers agonizing over how to tell America's story to the world. Each has his own pet theory, and our operations overseas reflect all kinds of personal prejudices. I had no idea that international communication had been reduced to such a science!"

Neither Conroy nor Vetter pretended to be a scientist

dealing with a discipline based on verifiable principles of human behavior. Still, it was clear that communication with foreign peoples had come a long way from the "full, fair picture of America." The post-mortem on Dave Weed's Meet the Critic session, for example, cast insights on the growing sophistication of the group in as tricky an area as existed in international affairs.

One trainee began by suggesting that Weed's difficulties stemmed from the unfortunate nature of his opening remarks, largely because he had underestimated the opposition. Vetter agreed. He was emphatic on the dangers an American confronted in dealing with a Marxist mind, honed on dialectics, vicious in twisting the most innocent remark to our disadvantage.

Conroy urged caution in dealing with any individual or group of unknown attitude. "It's usually sensible to be noncommittal at first, in a friendly way of course, but feeling out the other fellow, finding out what's on his mind. If he calls American culture debased, don't attempt an all-out defense. Ask a question or two to narrow his criticism down to something specific, and deal with this."

Trainees picked up another point from Weed's difficulties: the futility of "truth" or "facts" in changing anti-American stereotypes. "Personal experience," someone suggested, "is often not only more believable, but more understandable than a spate of statistics. In dealing with the racial question, especially, we would do better to relate the changes in the conditions of the Negro that we have observed in our lifetime than to make exaggerated claims."

Dave Weed protested. "But I wasn't making exaggerated claims! I was simply telling the truth."

Conroy's pipe wagged with his words. "I'm afraid that the most obvious truths to us often seem like exaggerated claims to others. An Indian simply may not comprehend that American Negroes enjoy the advantages you so accurately described. It just doesn't fit into his own experience."

Morelli added: "To hold people's attention, a good human interest angle is better than any amount of facts and figures. We learned that in radio and television years ago."

Weed was also faulted for asserting the principle of equality as a purely American concept. The error lay in the failure to establish equality as a concept sanctioned by many races of man, throughout the ages, and to identify America with a universally accepted human aspiration. One of the trainees was reminded of the Russian claims to having invented the automobile, the airplane, the telephone. "It offended us, not only as a violation of fact, but as a symptom of nationalism carried to insane excess. In referring to equality in purely American terms, we may be making the same mistake. Eight hundred years before Christ the Upanishads dealt with this idea. When an American puts equality purely in American terms, he's likely to offend a sensitive Indian. The result, instead of a shared value binding Indians and ourselves, is to drive us apart."

Dave Weed jumped to his feet. "Since when do Indians believe that all men are created equal?" he demanded. "Everybody knows that Indians believe just the opposite —that everyone is born and stays a member of his caste! Who do you think you're kidding by tying equality and untouchability together?"

Conroy agreed with the futility of reaching too hard

for universal values. At the same time, he questioned the "everybody knows" approach to intercultural matters. "As professionals in this field, are we safe in assuming that what 'everybody knows' corresponds with what actually is? What does 'everybody' really know about caste in India? Is caste a part of the Hindu religion, or simply a custom that has grown up over the centuries? What are present attitudes in India toward caste? May we not be dealing with the same discrepancy between ideals and the absence of complete fulfillment that we recognize in our own society?" Conroy tapped the ashes from his pipe. "Maybe it's our duty as careerists in this field to dig down to the wellsprings of other societies, rather than just repeat what 'everybody knows.' Maybe that's the difference between amateurs and pros in this intercultural communications business."

It was on the need to relate American ideals to the deepest convictions of the human race that the orientation course focused. Conroy reminded us that the word "communication" came from the Latin *communis,* meaning common. "When we communicate with others, we aren't trying to sell our ideas. We are trying to share ideas. We are trying to establish commonness with someone." And Vetter never tired of stressing the unique quality that set Agency personnel apart from every other American engaged in mass communication. "You are not Americans dealing with other Americans. You are dealing with *non-* Americans. You are not delivering entertainment and news to *American* audiences. Your business is *international* communication. Your job is to project a message that has credibility in terms of *other* peoples' values, and not solely in terms of ours."

Days were given to dissecting President Eisenhower's statement of the Agency's mission. Like the rest of the group, I was irked by Conroy's insistence on careful scrutiny of every word. After all, the mandate seemed more an idealization of the Agency's aims than an operational directive. But, in Dave Weed's words, Conroy was determined to make "a federal case" of the statement of mission. In time we began to realize the reasons for Conroy's persistence.

The purpose of the Agency, it appeared, was not to direct the world's verdict on any event or issue. Nor was it our job to hand down the truth, as though we alone were in possession of the truth. The task, rather, was "to submit evidence" to a foreign jury, committing the American case to the judgment of other peoples who, in their own way, were trying to ascertain the truth and who would render their own verdict.

Our audience, according to the President, was "peoples." Not just the educated, the rich, the privileged, the powerful, but *peoples:* the mass, the community as distinguished from any special class.

The job was not to pin American labels on mankind's most honored ideals, but to associate American objectives with these ideals, revealing our policies and actions in the light of the beliefs, experiences, and interests of Muslims, Hindus, Buddhists, and others.

Our duty was not simply to broadcast our aims abroad, but to establish where possible a mutual or reciprocal relationship between our aims and those of other peoples.

Our responsibility was not to send overseas *all* aspects of American life and culture, but mainly those that facilitated understanding of our objectives and policies, and that were relevant to mankind's aspirations for freedom, progress, and peace.

Vince Patton's handsome face was thoughtful. "The President's directive," he said, "hangs on USIS walls from here to Hong Kong. How many USIS officers truly understand its meaning is another matter. Consciously applied to our problems, it would lead to something far different from our present operation."

Dave Weed threw up his hands. "If we're supposed to do what the President says, a lot of us don't belong in this business. I'm just a simple, honest newspaperman out to tell the world about America. All this stuff about harmonizing with Hindus is over my head!"

For the first time, others began to entertain doubts about their qualifications. This was to be no easy-going holiday abroad at government expense. To explain America involved far more than a pleasant personality and a college education. Our task involved as much knowledge of other cultures as of our own. It was based on disciplines which few of us had really mastered. The entire process of human communication, superficially simple, turned out to have nuances we did not suspect.

Conroy and Vetter, for example, stressed a formula evolved by Dr. Wilbur Schramm, a social scientist whose book *The Process and Effects of Mass Communication* was a primer of our course. Schramm held that successful communication between peoples occurred according to a certain pattern. Originating with a source, a message was expressed by an encoder and transmitted to a decoder who received it, processed it, and passed it on to its final destination. Source, encoder, decoder, destination: each of the four elements was indispensable.

Thus, our task was to determine a relevant message drawn from the source, the American people; to encode it, presumably with knowledge of the people to whom the message was addressed; to identify the decoders best able to receive, process, and pass on the message; to insure that the message had significance to those who comprised its destination. The formula distinguished between the decoder and the destination. The decoder, while a part of the destination, was an instrument in the transmission process. The destination was the ultimate audience: by Presidential definition, "peoples."

Considerable discussion arose over this point. Vince Patton mentioned that, operationally, the Agency saw the destination of its message as "opinion leaders" in other societies: those who, by dint of wealth, education, or rank, controlled the situation in any given country.

Dave Weed added that Americans in USIS were too few to communicate with millions of people, many of them illiterate. "Besides," he insisted, "the masses simply don't matter."

Some of the younger people disagreed with this interpretation. "If that's what the President meant, that's what he would have said," was one viewpoint. According to another: "We can talk our heads off about the importance of the individual, but if we practice something else—if we let our technique get in the way of our principles—we throw away the premise that underlies the whole American case." Others pointed out that the designation of educated, wealthy, or world-minded men was certain to affect the message. It would necessarily be conceived and expressed on a higher plane than would be the case if the general public were envisaged as the audience. "It's like *The New York Times* and the *Daily News*. The paper reflects the readership."

Above all, many were doubtful about the ability of Americans to identify genuine molders of public opinion in other societies. Were they the upper-class intellectuals and politicians whom we tended to cultivate? Or might they be men and women, hidden in the mass, about whose existence and influence we knew nothing? Proponents of this thesis cited an essay in Schramm's book. Based on a study of an American community during a national election, it revealed that opinion leaders were not concentrated in the upper brackets of the population, but were located in almost equal proportion in every social group. Opinion leaders, moreover, were influential only at certain times, and with respect to certain matters, by virtue of the fact that they were empowered to be so by other members of their group. There was little overlap of leadership; a leader in one sphere was not apt to be influential in another sphere as well. Opinion leaders and the people they influence were very much alike, and typically belonged to the same primary groups of family, co-workers, and friends.

Conroy and Vetter led us into a study of how other nations had approached the basic issues involved in the decoder-destination discussion. Using work-papers prepared under the auspices of the Institute of Communications Research at the University of Illinois, we explored the propaganda theories of the Nazis, British, and Soviets.

"The Nazis," as the British viewed it, "loved propaganda too much to use it well." They pitched their propaganda toward the least intelligent in the audience, appealing to sentiment rather than to reason. Goebbels picked a few themes and repeated them constantly, presenting every issue in a one-sided way. He assumed that the bigger the lie, the more it would be believed. Manipulating anxieties, aggressions, and hopes, Nazi propaganda was based on an ideology repugnant to a democratic people. Its lesson lay mainly in the lethal possibilities of propaganda cynically conducted for ignominious ends.

If the Nazis loved propaganda, the British deplored it. For that reason, perhaps, they used it well. The basic aims were to create an impression of overwhelming objectivity, to achieve total credibility, and, when it really counted, to capitalize on this credibility by slipping in something serving the British cause. The audience comprised "respected leaders of opinion" who were supplied with relevant facts, leaving them to draw the right conclusions and to publicize them. The message was often deliberately aimed over the audience's head. Whether or not it was understood, didn't matter. What mattered was to win respect for Britain's political institutions, credibility for its claims, admiration for its culture. The British approach was civilized. In an anticolonial era, Britain's bid had to be more to the heads of men than to their hearts. It was hardly in a position to lead an egalitarian crusade.

Soviet strategy contrasted sharply with the British. Its basic premise was that the masses were the chief source of power, and ultimately irresistible. To arouse and direct the masses was the Communist goal. The Soviets were awake to the awesome reality of the popular franchise, common in newly independent states. They also understood the isolation of illiterates from the political machinery. In these two factors they saw their chance. Ferreting out areas in other societies where permanent tensions existed, where one class or another suffered from a sense of discrimination, where people hungered for food

or status or freedom, the Soviets presented the Communist
Party as the political instrument of the workers and peasants. Identifying mass movements begotten by history, the
Party placed its agents within them in positions of power,
and awaited the right time to strike paralyzing blows at
the existing order.

Intellectuals were key Communist targets. But their
function, in part, was to decode the complex Communist
ideology into the simplest ideas with the greatest appeal
to the many. Trotsky had said: "Slogans corresponding to
the acute need of a class and epoch themselves create
thousands of channels for their own dissemination." The
Soviets sought to devise a message with such appeal, and
of such simplicity, that an inner momentum carried it to
its destination. "Land and peace," "Bread, peace and liberty," "Jobs for all"—slogans such as these had an earthy
ring that echoed among the hungry, the landless, the unemployed. Identification with mass grievances gave communism its moral dynamism, its revolutionary power. In
the agitator's lexicon, truth had no meaning. "'Truth' is
partisan," Lenin had said. "Any idea of objective news is
nonsense and hypocrisy."

Like the Nazi, the Soviet apparatus was government-
directed and instantly responsive to any shift in the Party
line. But unlike the arrogant, egocentric Nazi, the Communist garbed himself in the raiment of his prey. "The
truth of Marxism," said Mao Tse-tung, "must be integrated
with the characteristics of the nation and given a definite
national form before it can be useful."

The Communist design went a long way toward convincing us that in designating "peoples" as the Agency's
audience, the President meant peoples and not simply the

upper classes. Any remaining doubt was dispelled by George Allen in a statement of his personal position, published at the time. In *Go Tell It to the People* the Agency's Director reviewed the changes in diplomacy over the twenty-eight years since he had entered the Foreign Service:

Once it was considered highly improper for one government to bypass another, and appeal directly to the people of another country for approval and support of its policies. . . . Today, the U.S. Information Agency is trying in every way to reach as many foreigners as possible. . . . During our present generation, peoples as individuals have become far more important in shaping national and international policies and actions. The importance of people, the dignity and worth of the individual, are basic tenets of the democratic faith . . . but curiously, the democracies were almost the last to adopt this new grass roots approach to foreign relations. The challenge of our century is breaking down the barriers that so long have separated the peoples of the world. With those barriers gone, the first great step will have been taken toward the primary objective of the "peoples" of the United Nations: "To save succeeding generations from the scourge of war."

About two thirds through the course, a note on the bulletin board requested that I call Personnel. Bad news had arrived from India. "The PAO in Delhi is dying. Fulminating hepatitis. You'd better plan to leave Washington within the week."

I called my wife in New Hampshire. Eadie broke the news to the kids. Jill, aged twelve, and Arthur, six, were Old Asia Hands. Bret, two, was eager for adventure. We arranged to meet at Idlewild airport the following Monday. Over lunch, I told Paul Conroy and Chuck Vetter how sorry I was not to complete the course. Conroy said that the only major area to be covered was American civilization.

"Don't worry about it," Conroy said. "Just remember what a Mexican once told me. 'We liked you Americans during your depression when you had problems and talked about them. But now you give the impression that you have no problems, only answers to other people's problems. It is hard for us to get along with such self-satisfied people, so different from ourselves.'"

Vetter added: "The great danger inherent in American civilization is its capacity to arouse envy, anger, despair in others. Too many of us forget that our mission overseas is not to encourage immigration to America. Our job is to make people want to stay at home, confident that they can pull themselves up by their own bootstraps."

I told them how much I had enjoyed the course. It had raised the Agency high in my estimation. But it hadn't provided any easy answers.

Conroy grinned. "Sorry," he said. "But the central fact of a free society is that it offers no canned solutions. The answer must be the individual's. It must flow from his mind, his will, his soul. No one can hand it to him. All we can do here is to help him in his struggle to find it."

I said good-by to the class. Then I went over to the Transportation Section to pick up the tickets for our flight, and to arrange for the shipment of our furniture and other effects to New Delhi. Lulu Lewis, a handsome colored woman, sat at a desk covered with airline ash trays, flags, and schedules. She had everything ready.

"You know what it's costing us taxpayers to send you, your family, and your belongings to India?" Lulu asked, her teeth flashing in a friendly smile. "Ten thousand dollars! Now mind, you better do a bang-up job!"

IV. Indian regimentals

The plane tore across the Tarmac and soared eastward to India. I unfastened my safety belt and tilted back the seat. My eyes closed, and as the engines raced forward, my mind slipped back—back to 1936, when India was still a British colony. I had arrived in Calcutta with a mixed bag of chores. *Esquire* magazine had commissioned a piece on "The Lure of the East." The *Herald Tribune* wanted a series on oriental bazaars. Included was one rather frivolous errand commanded by a friend, George McCurrach, a silk manufacturer in New York: to comb the country for designs and colors that might inspire new necktie fashions for men. As matters turned out, it was the search for the neckwear silks that opened windows on a colonial world that might otherwise have been, for me, forever shut.

The search began on Calcutta's main street, thronged with sacred cows and homespun-clad Bengalis. Suddenly a battalion of lancers trotted into view. Preceding the troops was a British major, caparisoned in a medal-splashed tunic, chalked breeches, and high Whitehall boots. It was his turban, however, that seized my eyes and imagination. Fold upon fold of striped silk—silver, gold, and crimson on a field of blue—crowned his head, with twin tails of silk fluttering behind in the breeze.

I followed the battalion to its barracks. Waiting until the major dismissed his men and dismounted, I walked up to him and came directly to the point. "Please, sir," I asked, "might I have a small swatch of your turban?"

The Guards moustache quivered. The blue eyes blazed. After a hasty explanation of my motive, however, they warmed with laughter. "How typically Yank!" he exclaimed, and invited me into the Mess.

Over whiskys, the major waxed enthusiastic. With the art of a haberdasher's clerk he twisted a tail of his turban to suggest a necktie's shape. "Smashing!" he said. "Just the thing to wear with mufti!"

Then, starting with his own brigade, he jotted down the names of regiments in the British Indian Order of Battle: the Rajputana Rifles, the Bikaner Camel Corps, the Mahratta Light Infantry, Hodson's Horse, the Sikh, Punjab, and Jat regiments, and others equally titillating to mind and tongue. Each, he said, had its own distinctive colors: gold and silver metallic threads embroidered on silks that spanned the rainbow's spectrum. To reach the regiments was the only difficulty the major foresaw. No central depot existed where swatches of all the turbans could be procured. To build my collection, I would have to search out the troops wherever they might be bivouacking, from the Khyber Pass to Cape Comorin, from Bengal to Bombay.

In horse-drawn shays and third-class railway carriages, on camel back and afoot, I plunged into Kipling's India. It was an India of Moghul fortresses and British cantonments, strategically sited at every point of potential disorder. It was an India of orderly enclaves—of, by, and for the whites—surrounded by infinite Hindu and Muslim oceans. It was an India of kingly consumption, all the more conspicuous against a background of bazaars and *bustees* where dwelt the half-starved, half-naked, seemingly half-human masses. It was, pre-eminently, an India of the masses. Innumerable, unkempt, inscrutable, they suffused the land with their sadness. Traveling to far-flung outposts of empire on my quest, I came to know them well. I slept on their rope-beds, ate their millet cakes, drank their tea, fed their fleas, and shared their melancholy.

One by one, from puzzled colonels and bemused quartermasters guarding Britain's distant frontiers, I gathered my collection of Indian Regimentals. And one by one, I gathered my memories of pre-independence India.

I remembered an Indian intellectual with an Oxford accent who had accosted me in Tamil Nad. He asked me to sign an anti-nautch petition. "What," I asked, "is nautch?" He said it was a licentious survival of India's barbaric past —a dance in which women immodestly moved their bodies in a carnal manner. "It has no place in modern India," he said. "Our English friends deem it a disgrace. The ignorant masses must be protected from it."

Days later, wandering about a bazaar, I was drawn by a drum beat to a tiny theater. For a few annas, a curtain was drawn and I went inside. It was filled with the ragtag of town and village, and stank of cheap cheroots. I squatted beside a soiled old man who introduced himself as a *guru*, a teacher. The drum was joined in a wild *raga* by the string instruments beloved of the people: a *veena*, a *tampura*, and a *sitar*. Across the stage eddied eight ravishing Devadasis, "servants of God," midriffs bare beneath tight *cholis*, limbs undulating under sheer *saris*.

Debased, denatured, and burlesqued, this was the three-thousand-year-old ritual temple dance of Vedic India. Some day it would be honored everywhere as Bharata Natyam, the dance of India. Throughout centuries of persecution by conquerors and prudes, the peasants had kept the dance alive in marriage and childbirth ceremonies, and in shabby music halls like this. To them it was known as nautch. To them it was thirty centuries of divine and human wisdom, derived from printed pages they could not read, and retold by the manipulation of fingers and toes, the movement of hip and thigh, the melody of *tampura* and *sitar*.

My Western senses perceived little at first but the exquisite beauty of the Devadasis. In their unabashed sexuality, the erotic temple frescoes of Khajurahoa came to life. Only gradually, assisted by the *guru*, did the subtler symbolism come into focus. "See the hands, sahib!" he hissed. "See the fingers!" Grudgingly moving my eyes from the half-moons bursting from their bodices, I obeyed. Peacocks, parrots, full-blown lotus leaves seemed, figuratively, to fall from the dancers' fingertips. Bees, swans, tridents formed magically at their feet. Men became gods, and gods descended to earth to dally with milkmaids.

> O Lord Krishna! I am on my way to sell buttermilk.
> Please let me go!
> I assure thee I shall come in the evening.
> Do not hold my skirt. Let me go!
> O Krishna, I implore thee not to tease me now.
> Please let go my hand! Why art thou so impatient!
> Krishna!

The *raga* ended. Heaven and earth were one. Body and soul were blissfully united. The world at last was blessed with *moksha*, liberation. The nymphs glided into the wings, thumbs and forefingers touching, the rest of the hand outstretched in a *mukala*, classic gesture of pleading.

There was pleading in the voice and manner of the old *guru* as we parted. "Please, sahib," he begged, "do not report what you have seen to your friends. Nautch belongs to the people. We have so little, yet even this they want to take away."

I remembered, weeks later, a hand appearing in the window of my train during a brief stop at a way station in the jungle. It belonged to a peasant woman, holding up her baby in one hand and begging alms with the other. Flies covered the infant's pallid face. Maggots pulsed under the eyelids. It was dead. I dropped a rupee into the woman's palm. Her thumb and forefinger touched, showing their tips. The rest of the hand was outstretched in a *mukala*, classic gesture of pleading.

I remembered the missionaries I had met in India. There was a young American in the Madura-Ramnad region who dressed, ate, and talked like his Tamil neighbors. Every day before dawn he was at work in the fields, hardly different from any peasant. In the cool of the evening, dozens of his Indian friends dropped by to exchange ideas about seed, cattle, irrigation, and religion.

"I came out," he confessed, "to convert the heathens. But the heathens taught me things about the fullness of Jesus Christ I never had known before. I've discovered Him in Hindu temples, in Muslim mosques, in every heart upturned toward God, regardless of how a faith is labeled.

I don't tell these people how to find God. I simply live as a Christian, speaking the truth as I know it, learning as much as I teach."

I remembered another missionary whose service I attended one Sunday. His sermon denounced Hinduism as a savage rite rather than a religion. After exalting his own faith, he lifted his voice in a hymn.

> From Greenland's icy mountains,
> From India's coral strand,
> Where Africa's sunny fountains
> Roll down the golden sand;
> From many an ancient river,
> From many a palmy plain,
> They call us to deliver
> Their land from error's chain.

I looked around to see those who had called him to deliver them from error's chain. Except for himself, his wife, and me, there was no one there.

I remembered a naked man walking down the Janpath in New Delhi. Passersby seemed indifferent, but never before had I seen an unclothed adult walking down a public thoroughfare. Moved to pity, I pressed a rupee into his hand. He looked at the bill with vacant eyes and resumed his walk without a word, holding the money awkwardly in his fingers. Suddenly a vagrant darted from behind a tree, seized the bill and disappeared in the bazaar. I gave chase, cornering him in a teahouse. Curious people gathered; a policeman intervened. I said the thief had stolen the poor man's money.

"But he is a Thug," cried someone in the crowd, referring to the community from which the culprit came. "He steals because God wills it. He must do his religious duty."

The victim agreed. "Besides," he said, "I am not poor. The universe is my treasure."

A woman pointed a finger at me. "Only a fool," she shrieked, "would give money to a man without a pocket in which to put it!"

I walked away, awed by the width of the gulf I had just witnessed.

I remembered a week end at a Maharajah's palace. Crimson-sashed coolies led me to my suite. Walls, floors, and ceilings were of smoked crystal. Tables, chairs, dressers, bed—even the bathroom bidet—were also of glass, pieced together from millions of prisms by a Belgian *vitrerie* and imported at incalculable cost. Whenever I moved, a chain reaction set every mirror in motion. Wherever I looked, my eyes stared back in an infinity of receding reflections. What manner of man, I wondered, was the Maharajah.

He turned out to be a splendid specimen, educated at Cambridge, tailored by Savile Row, and indistinguishable from his British guests except for the number and size of his imperial Orders. At dinner his conversation matched the menu, both consisting of peafowl, plover, pigeon, partridge, pheasant, duck, and boar. Brandies in hand, we trailed His Highness through twenty of the two hundred rooms in the palace. It was a taxidermist's dream, with overtones of Sotheby's and the Smithsonian. The Maharajah seemed indifferent to his priceless possessions until, in his den, he paused before a galaxy of jeweled frames enshrining autographed portraits of the British royal family. Lifting his glass, the Maharajah intoned: "To the King!"

We rose early next morning for a hunt. A buffalo was

tethered in a jungle clearing. The guests loitered in treetop aeries, consuming champagne, waiting for tiger to catch the quarry's scent. I shared a *machan* with a British brigadier, a friend of the major in Calcutta to whose good offices I owed this taste of oriental opulence. He was a jovial giant with long experience of India. To him its enchantment lay largely in opportunities to hunt gaur, saladang, leopard, black antelope, and the fierce wild boar. He talked lovingly of trouting along a Kashmir beat, of skiing the Kandahar, of living a life few Englishmen with his income could enjoy at home.

To me, the wonder of India was how a handful of Englishmen such as the brigadier could rule so vast, so populous, so mysterious a land.

A monocled eye looked to see if we were out of earshot. Reassured, he leaned close. "Single out the leaders," he confided, "the handful of natives who really count—the Maharajahs, the upper classes, the rich, the educated, the ambitious. Waste no time on the rabble. They do as they're told."

The brigadier mopped a bead of champagne from his moustache. "The rest is easy. Flatter the leaders with titles and medals. Bribe them with Rolls Royces. Frighten them now and then with a flypast of Moths, or with a whiff of rumor that a rival is inching up in Whitehall's favor. Play them off against each other. In a word, divide and conquer."

At sundown a tiger leaped upon the screaming buffalo's back and broke it with the sweep of a paw. Shots rang out and the tiger dropped. The court photographer snapped a group picture with the prize. Elephants moved up to bear us back to the palace.

It was harvest time and, though darkness was descending, blind-folded buffalos, hitched to millstones, were walking in rings, grinding the grain. We came to a field where a man and woman dug their shoulders into a buffalo's harness, plodding round and round, staining the millet with a circle of sweat. On impulse, I asked the mahout to halt, and watched until the couple paused to rest.

"*Kisan*," I called. "Farmer, where is your animal?" The man was shy, or didn't understand.

The woman answered. "Our son is sick. We needed money for prayer and medicine. We sold our buffalo to the Maharajah for his hunt!"

I remembered another Englishman, a lean, bespectacled professor on leave from the University of London. We shared a coach compartment crossing the Western Ghats. "Humbug," he said when I repeated the divide-and-conquer doctrine of his countryman. "Britain has neither divided nor conquered India. Our central government, our civil service, our language and schools, our trains and trunk roads—above all, our unpopularity—have unified India as never before. As for conquering India, fiddlesticks! Neither the Persians, Scythians, Saracens, Greeks, Afghans, Huns, Mongols, or Moghuls succeeded. Nor have we. Yes, we have seduced a few of their princes. The upper classes have always aped the culture of the invader. In doing so, they usually lose their credentials of leadership. As for the Hindu masses, they remain unconquered. The only leadership to which they respond is one that speaks for them, the people."

I asked the secret of Hindu survival. "Centuries before Christ," the professor replied, "Vedic scripture gave these people a social organization stressing the individual's duties rather than his rights. It laid down laws governing

every action, from the cleaning of one's anus after defeca-
tion to the conduct of foreign affairs. Anything so old tends,
in time, to become corrupted. The exaggerations of caste,
idol worship, child marriage—these pollute the purity of
the original scripture. But Hinduism survives because it is
resilient. It has absorbed every idea from the divinity of
kings to the Social Contract, molding them all into a religion with deep meaning to the masses. Today, such leaders
as Gandhi and Tagore are reviving Vedic belief, building
social reforms around it, making it the mainspring of Indian nationalism."

Our train crawled past a Hindu village. A haze of smoke
from a thousand dung fires hung over the hovels. A hum
compounded of children's cries, the lowing of cattle, the
squealing of ox carts, the pounding of tools upon wood,
brass, and leather filtered into the coach, carrying with
it the smell of excrement. I confessed my bafflement at the
scene outside. None of the order, the wisdom, the majesty
of which my companion spoke was visible in this bedlam.

The professor shrugged. "All the same," he said, "there,
in that village, the future of India is being formed. Everything depends on our ability to see the things of value that
lie beneath the rubbish. The first Englishmen who came
to India had the vision. James Prinsep decoded the people's alphabet. Sir William James translated the *Code of
Manu*, Kautilya's *Art of Politics*, all the great Hindu epics
—not simply as a cultural exercise, but for the East India
Company's official use. Young men coming out from England were forced to read them. Sir Warren Hastings left
newcomers in no doubt about their mission: 'to convince
the peasant that you will stand between him and the hand
of oppression . . . to teach him a veneration and affection
for the humane maxims of our government.' Those early

Englishmen—Munro, Elphinstone, Metcalf, Malcolm—took India less by force of arms than by their familiarity with Hindu thought and custom."

The professor shook the dust from his solar topee and clapped it back on his head. "But times have changed. Today the Englishman in India seals himself inside his own Western-built institutions. Through indirect rule, he has cut himself off from the people. And so the mighty British Raj will lose India to a shrunken, half-naked mummy of a man who understands and speaks for his people."

I remembered the shrunken, half-naked mummy of a man who understood and spoke for his people. A pony-cart bounced me to his *ashram* in Segaon. He was holding a garden meeting where people came to gain his blessing. Despite distance, heat, and plague, they had come in scores. A lone constable stood outside the gate with an iron-tipped club symbolizing imperial authority. Beyond, in the doorway of a mud-walled hut, sat Gandhi. Sighting him for the first time, I stood stock still. It seemed incredible that British power could be challenged by this little man in a wrinkled *dhoti*.

One of the Mahatma's followers separated himself from the crowd. He led me to a shadowed place beneath a tree, and translated Gandhi's words into excellent English. I made no notes, but my memory of his remarks was later refreshed by excerpts from Gandhi's writings.

Gandhi was talking about something he called *Sarvodaya*, "the welfare of all." "I want wealth in the hands of all. The rich man will be left in possession of his wealth. He will use what he reasonably requires for his personal needs, and will act as a trustee for the remainder to be used for society."

Gandhi restated his points in Hindu parables. "We will remember how the Lord Krishna in the Bhagavad Gita showed to Arjuna that his enemies were self-destroyed by their own evil." The heads of the people wagged from side to side in India's gesture of assent. "Inequality is an evil, but I do not believe in eradicating evil from the human breast at the point of a bayonet. Violence is wrong because it overlooks the fact that evil can never be overcome by evil; it ceases only with good. As the means, so the end."

Gandhi leaned back against a bolster and closed his eyes for several seconds. "Everything," he resumed, "depends on the human individuality. I look upon any increase in the power of the State with the greatest of fear. It does the greatest harm to mankind by destroying individuality which lies at the root of all progress. The salvation of India lies in the labor, dignity, and freedom of its common people."

Gandhi looked at the nickeled watch that dangled incongruously from his *dhoti*. "The pilgrimage to independence," he concluded, "is a painful climb. It means penetration into the villages solely for the service of the villagers. It means education for the masses. It means an awakening national consciousness among the masses. It will not spring like a magician's mango. It will grow almost unperceived, like a banyan tree."

My friend invited me into the coolness of the house. A woman brought us buttermilk. I told him how touched I was by Gandhi's presence. As for his program, many of Gandhi's ideals were becoming American realities. America was practicing much that Gandhi preached.

My host agreed. "Much of Gandiji's thinking is influenced by your country. He reads the New Testament, and reveres Lincoln and Thoreau. America gained independence from England. This is an inspiration to Indians. It gives us confidence that we too some day shall be free."

I shook my head. "From what I've seen of India," I said, "the odds against independence seem too great."

"What have you seen of India?"

I spoke of the vastness of the subcontinent, of the multiplicity of its races and religions, of the diversity of its tongues, and of the advantages these factors conferred on the handful of powerful men who commanded the country's communications. I contrasted the poverty of the people with the wealth, education, and influence of the ruling classes, allied with the British. I spoke, above all, of the army I had come to know so well in my search for Indian Regimentals—an army meticulously trained, magnificently officered, abundantly supplied, formidably armed. "Is spirituality," I asked, "a match for such material power?"

The man's lips moved as if he were tasting my words. When he finally spoke, it was almost as if to himself. "May it not be that it is the British who are spiritual, and we the wielders of material power? May it not be that their Christian ethic, their sense of decency, the goodness within the English people may cause their government to give way? May it not be that in the weakness of five hundred million human beings the world will discover a new dimension of power? The odds against us indeed are long. But not, perhaps, so long as you think."

As I left the *ashram,* the constable snapped to attention, performing an elbow-cracking salute. My friend said farewell in the Indian fashion, pressing palm against palm in a *namaste.*

"My name is Vinoba Bhave," he said. "If I can ever be of service, come again."

My next visit to India came ten years later. The war was over in Europe and I was ordered east to Chungking. Bad weather over the Hump bequeathed me a week end in Calcutta. Warships anchored in the Hooghly sent their smoke over a city stiff with soldiers and sailors of the Allied armies and fleets, celebrating the Japanese surrender with a parade of men and machines of modern war that numbed one with their menace.

That night, from my hotel window, I watched three American sailors roll out of a bar and shout obscenities at a half-caste girl. Her Indian escort objected and a burly gunner struck him in the face. From the shadows, suddenly, phantoms surrounded the sailors. There was an agonized American oath, a white jacket stained red. The other two fought fiercely, but within minutes, they lay on the sidewalk in puddles of blood.

Two jeeps pulled up, loaded with British and American shore patrols, Sten guns ready. Except for the three bleeding men, the street was empty. There was something defiant in the silence: something mocking of the West, of white men, of machines of modern war.

Whatever the reason—the war, the mounting intensity of the independence movement, new pan-Asian impulses generated by the Japanese—there was in India in 1945 a truculence I had not encountered before. I sensed it in the undergraduates who cornered me during a visit to their campus. "You are an American," one said, pointing to my uniform. I nodded. A barrage of questions burst over me. "Why did you drop atom bombs on Eastern people and not on the Germans?" "Why is America an ally of the imperialist powers?" "Why doesn't President Roosevelt force Churchill to give India independence?"

Patiently I put forward America's position. It was overwhelmed by waves of disbelief. One youngster proved me wrong with a long recitation from the Ramayana. Another quoted Subhas Chandra Bose, a man about whom I knew no more than I did of the ancient epic. Another placed his face close to mine and shouted, "You are an imperialist! You are ignorant of any viewpoint but your own! And to cover up your crimes, you lie!"

I said I told the truth. A student looked at me with pity. "Only by knowing the Infinite Being can man know truth. Tell us, sahib, are only Americans acquainted with the Infinite Being?"

I became conscious, in 1945, of a new India, a challenging India, an India which would not be taken for granted or patronized. It was an India impatient of Western argument, asserting and insisting on values of its own, pitting the speed and stealth of little men against the might of empire.

It was an India aware of a new dimension of power.

My wife's first impressions of India were formed in 1951, after independence and partition. East Pakistan refugees thronged the park across the street from our hotel. Covered by white shrouds, they stretched endlessly in the sun, looking and smelling like the dead. Eadie covered her eyes and cried, "Let's go away! I can't stand India!"

We left Calcutta, only to find ourselves amidst a famine in Madras. In the diningroom of the Connemara Hotel, liveried bearers brought dishes hardly more than stained with a bilious green broth and a sliver of boiled mutton. Eadie was pregnant. She retched at the fare, blaming it on her condition. But the real reason, I knew, was the horde of starving children haunting the gardens outside the hotel.

It was better in the villages than in the cities. One village especially made a happy impression—a village where children went to school. School was a *peepul* tree. The blackboard was the earth. The chalk was a stick of wood with which the pupils scratched words and numbers on the ground.

The headman was proud. "This is the new India," he said. Eadie pointed to a ten-year-old boy tending a flock of geese beside the village pond.

"Why isn't he at school?" she asked.

"He is already educated," the headman replied. "He can count. We can trust him not to lose our geese."

Eadie collapsed in Bombay. A bed was found for her in the Northcote Nursing Home behind the Taj Mahal hotel. The Indian staff struggled to save her life and the unborn baby's. Through their efforts and with the help of medicine provided by friends in the USIS, she was out of danger. Leaving her to convalesce, I continued my work elsewhere in India.

My mission took me to many places I had known before independence. Although the high hopes ushered in with freedom had been clouded by the deaths of Gandhi and countless others who perished in Hindu-Muslim strife, India pulsed with a new spirit. People were hungry, but proud. The suffocating sadness of colonial India had been lifted.

Americans were playing a role small in scope, big with promise. I remembered a northern village where Indians and Americans, joint members of a team, had induced farmers to plant a new strain of wheat called Punjab 591. The crop prospered, and the villagers accepted other innovations: an iron plow, a harrow with a light wooden frame and iron teeth, a longer sickle. A cooperative union was revived and small-scale industry devoted to the manufacture of charcoal, tools, and tiles began to flourish. Old wells were cleaned, and new paths were laid to outside markets. To fatten the cattle, fields were planted with *berseem*, a rich grass that increased milk yields by a third. Working side by side, Americans and Indians were harvesting rich crops in both food and friendship.

I remembered another village in the Pipri district where an American expert had come to teach the people to grow better cotton. "Do exactly what I say," he had warned. "Remember, I make more money than Mr. Neeroo!" The people were compliant. There was a good monsoon and the fields flowered. The American was proud of the crop. Whereas the native seed had produced long, coarse stalks with meager bolls, the new seed yielded large white puffs almost too heavy for the stalks to sustain. The American departed, warning the villagers not to mix the old seed with the new.

Next year he returned. Coarse-stemmed, small-bolled cotton spotted the fields. Furious, he demanded an explanation.

"Sahib," the headman said, "our *desi* seed gives us both cotton for our clothing and coarse stems with which we thatch our homes. Your seed gives nothing but cotton. Cotton is not enough. A man needs shelter too."

I returned to Bombay heartened by the new India. I was joyous, too, at Eadie's recovery. She had regained some of her lost weight, and all her high humor. Doctors and nurses flocked into the room to share the pleasure of our reunion. Later, when we were alone, Eadie told me that, unknown to her, they had contributed part of their own meager rations to make sure she had enough.

The nurses drove out to the airport to say farewell. The taxi driver, a gigantic Sikh, lifted Eadie gently and carried her into the plane. I reached into my pocket. Not a rupee was left. "Sorry," I said, "I have no money."

"Never mind, sahib," he said, in well-accented English. "It is an honor to serve an old comrade-in-arms."

I was puzzled by his remark until, noting his eyes fixed on a point below my chin, I looked down. I was wearing an Indian Regimental necktie, the colors of the Sikh Regiment. I pulled it off and placed it, like a garland, around his neck. A great smile broke through the blackness of his beard. He waved to me as I entered the plane. It was half salute, half *namaste*.

"Bring back the *chota sahib* someday!" the head Sister begged. "After he is born, bring the baby back to India!"

"I will," Eadie promised gratefully, "I will, I will!"

Her promise would soon come true.

v. The collision

Birds awakened me. With ardent burbling, two pigeons were mating in the transom above the bathroom door. Outside, a pair of kingfishers scolded a clutter of crows. Framed in the window, low in the morning sky, great skeins of graylag geese commuted from the Jumna River to the Gurgaon Lakes. From a fan blade suspended over my head, a sparrow watched me with beady eyes. Amid wisps of straw stuck in the metal cup that held the fan pole to the ceiling, six tiny beaks were visible. They opened in a shrill chorus each time the mother bird flew up with a crumb. Following her flight to the table beside my bed, I discovered that the bearer had brought my *chota hazri*—two biscuits and a cup of tea on which the sparrow and her brood were already feeding. I brushed a fleck of feather off a biscuit and lay back against the bolster, nibbling, luxuriating in the coolness of the Indian dawn, reflecting on the miracle of India's birds. Nowhere on earth were birds so fecund and fearless.

We had arrived in Delhi late the night before, after an

arduous trip. Eadie and the children were sleeping off the sedative with which they had been drugged; she needed all the rest she could get before beginning the search for permanent quarters. I slipped on a robe and went into the bathroom. It overlooked a settlement of squatters—taxi drivers and their families who served the Cecil Hotel. The sun's first rays lit up the purple jacarandas under which bearded men lay stretched. Women were already at work, roasting wheat cakes over dried-mud stoves. Smoke mingled with the mist; the pleasantly bitter smell of burning wood spiced the fragrance of flowers. Sweet peas, larkspur, foxglove, asters, phlox—amid their glory a woman squatted, brown bottom bare. Bottle flies buzzed over the droppings.

The Cecil's diningroom had made no concessions to India's independence. Everything was as colonial as on my earlier visits. The same English hunting scenes adorned the walls. The same silver-plated cruets weighted the tables. The same blue-eyed Boniface, Pauline White, greeted the guests and lovingly bullied the servants. Ali, Ajit, Gobind, Ram, and the rest, like superannuated interns in their spotless long-coats, still grooved the mosaic floors with bare feet, as flat as ever. As for the fare, the boiled milk was as clotted, the kippers as tart, the toast as cold as English taste demanded. Beside my plate lay the same papers: the *Statesman,* the *Times of India,* the *Hindustan Times.* All bore the British mastheads, the Fleet Street format, the Queen's English of another epoch. Only the news heralded an India that began beyond the Cecil's gate.

A Ford station wagon was waiting to take me to the office. The driver was a bone-thin Muslim boy named Sadiq. Traffic kept to the left, mostly students cycling toward Delhi University and St. Stephan's College, their back seats burdened with text books, tiffin tins, or pretty coeds. Monkeys gamboled in the old English cemetery. Lichen-covered tombstones marked the graves of men who died in the great Indian uprising of 1857. An empire lay interred with their bones.

Vehicles queued outside Kashmir Gate, the narrow entrance into the city. We waited while a camel caravan disputed passage with a Mercedes Benz bus. A two-toned Pontiac raced up and pushed impatiently into the melee. Camels and cursing men gave way and, horn blaring, the car darted into Elgin Road. Sadiq eased the Ford through the arch and maneuvered among the merchants fringing the twisted streets. Omens of approaching summer were everywhere. Pushcarts laden with long thin cucumbers competed with sugar cane crushers dispensing juice. Potters from Sabzimandi presided over mountains of earthen vessels for chilling water. In open stalls, secretarial students pecked at typewriters; a venereal disease quack dispensed drugs; sweating salesmen unfolded bolts of filmy gauze for summer *saris*.

Carpenters, wheelwrights, and tailors worked out of doors, controlling intricate tools with agile toes. Crowding them were idlers, astrologers, Brahman bulls, barbers, and dealers in plastic combs, glass bangles, brassieres, sandals, spectacles, old iron, spoiled fruit, and chromolithographs of Brahma, Siva, Gandhi, and Nehru. Radios trumpeted hybrid tunes from the latest Hindi movie hits, half *alaap*, half rock'n'roll. Overhead spread the bead trees, the "Pride of India." Their sweet-scented blossoms perfumed the fetid air, not quite hiding the stench of a pie-dog rotting outside an al fresco restaurant serving *dosas*, Indian blinis from Bangalore.

We passed the Red Fort, shimmering in the rising heat.

Built three centuries before by Shah Jehan, the citadel was now the communications hub of the Indian army. A troop of motorcyclists gyrated across the plain, training for a tattoo to be held a few days hence—a full-dress affair with bagpipes, sham battles, and a flight of jets. The meadow was a mecca for gypsy puppeteers, dancing bears, and musicians rehearsing marches with horns and drums rented from stalls in the Silver Market across the street. On the sward sat Hindu holy men, naked except for strings around their loins and ash smears on their foreheads, oblivious to soldiers, musicians, and the Jama Masjid, the Cathedral Mosque, Islam's largest, silhouetted against the sun. Under its ramparts huddled the junk dealers of Delhi, the ancient Kabaris, part of the history of the Mosque, whose ancestors had worked there in Moghul times as *bhishtis,* water boys, and who had claimed sanctuary ever since. Pilgrims bowed before the lofty minarets, under one of which reposed a henna-dyed hair from the beard of the Prophet.

At Delhi Gate the highway widened. The debris of construction strewed the streets, with here and there a shovel banging into stone images dating back ten centuries. Petrol stations, crowding the ruins of crumbling temples, advertised "Be Sure with Shell." Above scarlet cotton trees, modern concrete buildings stood on stilts. Their louvered windows and frescoed walls turned their backs on Shah Jehan's moats and minarets. Shops were windowed with glass, and staffed with clerks in Western dress. Moving picture palaces blazed with posters. One marquee featured a recumbent, half-nude blonde starring in the newest American import. Beside it, over a book stall, a huge sign said: "Read Soviet Books."

In front of hotels stood majestically moustached doormen in exaggerated Hindu dress, with turbans proud as peacocks. Like so many scattered petals, women were here and there on the lawns, manicuring them with sickles, scavenging grass and bundling it into bags to sell as fodder. Tourists were already about, haggling with Nepalese souvenir vendors over dubious Buddhas spread on the ground in the shadow of golden *neem* trees. As Sadiq plunged into Connaught Place, I glimpsed the gentle Mongol smiles that hid fraudulence deeper than any Yankee trader's.

Connaught Circus, named after the last surviving son of Queen Victoria, was New Delhi's hub. All roads led to its arcade-shadowed shops. Here, physically as well as figuratively, centuries and cultures clashed. As though to prove the point, the two-toned Pontiac that had passed us at Kashmir Gate stood stalled amid an excited crowd, a front fender crumpled. Beside it a buffalo quivered dumbly in a pool of blood. The two drivers, one a slight Hindu with close-cropped head and top-knot, the other a big crew-cut American, put their conflicting claims to a puzzled policeman. Sadiq asked a bystander what had happened. In a gush of angry Urdu the man explained that the car had dashed down the wrong side of the road, slashing the buffalo. The animal had bolted, catching its horns in the fender. "Someone," the man shouted, "should tell the sahibs to have a care!"

A policeman waved us on. Sadiq turned into the Janpath and pulled up before a four-story building numbered 54. The Stars and Stripes drooped above the entrance. A sign read "United States Information Service." A cocoa-colored man in a dirty *dhoti* thrust a card into my hand. "Salaam, sahib," he babbled, his eyebrows arching until they disappeared into his turban. "You are a tumbleweed, sahib. Be careful. You will be blown back and forth by the wind.

Only I can guarantee delights and riches, and sweeten your future with melted butter! Please sahib . . ."

I walked up three flights to the office. A *sari*-clad receptionist was addressing envelopes at the desk in the foyer. Water colors of the Washington Monument, the White House, and Mount Vernon brightened the ochre walls. A rack of pamphlets flanked a sofa. On a table lay copies of the *American Reporter,* a fortnightly tabloid of Indo-American news launched seven years before. The PAO's office had hardly changed since the time of my last visit. Adorning the wall was a framed photograph of Prime Minister Nehru looking sourly at Tom Two Arrows, an American Indian in beads, feathers, and war paint, brought to Delhi by USIS some months before to perform tribal dances. A teak bookshelf, burdened with titles found only in government offices, faced a desk covered by a sheet of cracked plate glass. Behind the desk sat a thin man in his early forties, his dark hair swept back from a high forehead, nostrils flaring from a Castillian beak.

"Say," he said, drawing the word out into three syllables, "welcome to the sweatshop!" He leaped up, darted around the desk and, pumping my arm, introduced himself as Tom Allen, the Cultural Affairs Officer. The girl with the notebook at his side was Jane Williams, the American secretary. Her gray eyes, behind harlequin glasses, warmed me with their welcome.

I asked about the condition of Helen Semmerling, my predecessor. Tom said she was still in coma at Holy Family Hospital. For the first time, however, the Embassy doctor felt she had a fighting chance for life. Tom was serving as Public Affairs Officer pro tempore. Without delay, he briefed me on the local situation.

India, he explained, was divided into four consular Districts: Bombay, Calcutta, Madras, and New Delhi. USIS maintained posts in each. Delhi, too, was the home of USIS-India. Under the Country Public Affairs Officer, it commanded the entire USIS operation in the subcontinent. Its offices were located on the other side of town, near the local golf course. To avoid confusion with our own shop, USIS headquarters was generally referred to as Golf Links.

Our office, Delhi Branch Post, served an area including the States of Rajasthan, the Punjab, and Uttar Pradesh, and two Union Territories, Delhi and Himachal Pradesh, ruled by the Central Government. Flanked by Pakistan in the West, Bihar in the east, Bombay in the south and, in the north, by Kashmir, Nepal, and Tibet, the area occupied 304,078 square miles, about a quarter of the subcontinent's land mass. Within the District dwelt 110 million of India's 420 million souls. All in all, Tom said, it was the largest area of USIS responsibility in the world.

It was also one of the most complex. About eighty million of the people were Hindus, eleven million were Muslims, six million were Sikhs. The rest were Jains, Buddhists, Christians, Jews, or members of other sects. Four major languages were spoken: Hindi, Urdu, Rajasthani, and Punjabi. About English there was disagreement. Some felt it was diminishing year by year in quality and use; others believed it was becoming more important. New Delhi itself was the capital of a country that seemed, on the surface, stable. New steel mills, dams, irrigation and hydroelectric schemes were fleshing out the Five Year Plans. Industrial and agricultural output were the best on record.

Nevertheless, Tom saw little cause for complacency. 28,400 new Indians were born every day; half of India's gains were erased by population increase. Mass misery resisted Five Year Plans, foreign aid, and other measures to allay it. Consumer prices had risen 15 per cent since 1956. Committed to a "socialist pattern of society," India knew neither the productivity of a free economy nor the forced results of a fettered economy. Unemployment, caste discrimination, corruption, and other ills persisted, discrediting democracy as a sensible solution to India's problems.

Literacy was spreading. Perhaps two adults in ten could read and write. But knowledge whetted rather than allayed the people's appetite for betterment of their material condition. Living standards were improving. But to an impatient people the tempo seemed too slow. Benefits seemed to accrue to a privileged few rather than to the destitute many. Indian youth especially was in crisis. Alienated from its elders, it had found no world of its own. The past was receding; the future was shapeless. The result was rebellion against authority, an urge to identify with anybody or anything against the *status quo*.

Chief beneficiary of popular dissatisfaction with democratic leadership was the Communist Party. It worked close to the grass roots, championing the underdog and fanning discontent on local issues. Recruiting strength among farmers, workers, students, and intellectuals, its cadres drove toward the long-range goal: a Communist India. Already it had captured one state, Kerala, by popular vote.

Asked how people felt about the United States, Tom said: "Our personal relationships with Indians couldn't be better. In fact, some officers believe that good will between India and America is at an all-time high. But surveys don't bear them out."

Jane Williams disappeared into her cubbyhole adjoining the office, and returned with two memoranda. One was a survey of student opinion entitled "Indian Images of America." Conducted by the Center for International Studies of the Massachusetts Institute of Technology, it characterized America as "a highly unequal, oppressive, conformist, and bacchanalian society of rich and poor, white and colored, drunkenness and divorce, all highlighted by an apparently hypocritical contrast with our ostensible principles of equality and democracy."

Life in America was seen by Indians as a boom-and-bust affair. The country was run by big business. Totally unplanned, our economy suffered chronically from overproduction and unemployment. The solution to these problems was sought in foreign markets, creating fears in Indian minds of a new American imperialism.

Students thought of the United States as a warlike nation. Some believed Americans might stumble into war because our economy was geared to war production, and because our ruling circles were militaristic. Others believed we were just biding our time and would launch a war to destroy communism whenever we thought we could do so with impunity. Anticommunism was considered to be the only objective of American foreign policy.

The deplorable status of the American Negro figured largely in India's image of America; 13 per cent of those interviewed thought American Negroes were slaves. Some Indian students said they would never visit America. "All dark skinned people are in danger of being lynched."

While Americans were deemed materialistic, sexually loose, and lucky in having fallen heir to natural resources that made the country rich, the Russian, according to the MIT report, "was the epitome of the virtuous citizen— hard working, brave, strong, patriotic, honest, progressive, and peace loving. A minority of Indians pointed to the cruelty of the Soviet regime, but without ever using the word dictatorship. Altogether, not more than 15 per cent had anything negative to say about the USSR."

The MIT report identified the major American error:

Our own attempts to sell the United States have often stressed exactly the wrong things. For example, we were proud of our good life, and did not consider ourselves materialistic because we tried to achieve a high standard of living. This standard of living was one of the things we had advertised most widely. It was, of course, envied in India, but envy of it did not mean admiration for the people who had it. Knowledge of our living standards had fed the image of ourselves as happy bon vivants with enormous power, not the image of ourselves as hard working and frugal in the struggle for a better community.

Jane's second memorandum disclosed the results of a public opinion poll recently completed in India's larger cities. It accented a catastrophic drop in America's stock since Sputnik. India's basic interests were linked with China and the Soviet Union. Despite almost two billion dollars of American aid—and only a pittance from Moscow—most respondents cited Russia as India's "real best friend." In Indian minds, both Russia and China were more sincere than America in their desire for peace and disarmament. Indeed, while the USSR and China rated praise as being anticolonial, the United States ranked with Britain as an imperialist power. Asked "Which system will win out in peaceful competition?" and "Which nation is ahead in science?" Indians voted against America two to one. As for the economic system Indians favored, socialism and communism led. While the United States was

mentioned more than Russia as a land of economic opportunity, capitalism as a means to Indian progress was condemned.

Tom explained that India's resentments against the
United States were largely rooted in India's dispute with
Pakistan over Kashmir. Coupled with American arms aid
to Pakistan, our refusal to champion India's claim created
an impression that the United States favored the Pakistani
position. Certain remarks by Secretary of State Dulles,
seeming to support Lisbon's claims on Goa, furthered the
conviction that America's policies hindered rather than
helped to advance India's legitimate aspirations. Involved
in both matters was the issue of collective security. America's partiality to military pacts, some of which included
Pakistan and Portugal as members, underlay the Indian
belief that America prized the olive branch less than the
sword.

Both polls reflected the opinions of India's educated
classes. I asked Tom where the masses of farmers and
workers stood. Tom shot his cuffs and shrugged. "We have
very little contact with the masses. We know almost nothing about them. But it's out there in the *mofussil*"—a Kip-
lingesque term for the countryside to which Tom was ad-
dicted—"that the Communists are making hay!"

Anticipating my next question, Jane placed before me a
statement of Delhi Post's assets. Considering the population of the District, the complexity of its cultures, and the
obloquy attaching to the American position, they didn't
seem great. In manpower we numbered eight Americans
and fifty-five Indians, including receptionists, chauffeurs,
file clerks, sweepers, and other nonproductive personnel.
It was the budget, however, that made me wince. To reach
110 million people for a year on all problems affecting rela-

tionships between India and the United States, the dollars allotted to Delhi Post were less than the amount spent promoting a single sexy American film in India.

An incurable optimist, Tom added that our position was strengthened by a variety of positive factors. The Ambassador and other American officials in New Delhi were active influences in the capital. Golf Links also supported the Post. About 40,000 copies of the *American Reporter* circulated in the District, about half in English and half in Hindi. A USIS book translation program had sold about a half-million copies of American titles in Hindi, Urdu, and Punjabi. Two USIS libraries, one in New Delhi and the other in Lucknow, served thousands of readers every month.

From Washington came a daily wireless file of news, a variety of press materials, photographs, exhibits, books, and films. Lecturers, entertainers, artists, and teachers were part of an exchange that brought human evidence of American civilization to India. Hundreds of Indians, returning from American universities, were sprinkled throughout the District, presumably advocates of our way of life. As for the Voice of America, no firm figures existed on listenership. With 350,000 receivers in the area, however, some short wave reception was assumed to occur. Locally, Golf Links' radio specialist was placing American talks and music on All-India Radio.

American aid made a crucial contribution. Interest payable by the Indian government on American wheat loans was being respent in India on higher education. Over a million dollars of this wheat loan money had been expended in Delhi District, principally on equipment and textbooks for universities and schools.

Private organizations were also active. The Ford Foun-

dation was an enormous force in improving Indian agriculture and small-scale industry. The U.S. Educational
Foundation in India was placing Indian teachers and students in American schools. American church organizations
and commercial concerns operated in the area. Nor could
those peripatetic American products, the tourist and the
Hollywood movie, be overlooked. Both entered India in
numbers unequaled by any other nation. Whether for
good or evil, their influence was strong.

Above all, the United States government and people
back home spawned the fundamental stuff of which America's image was made. Triumphs and defeats in the fields
of science, labor, economics, race relations, politics, foreign affairs, literature, and art—these brightened or black-
ened America's reputation. In Tom's words: "Propaganda
can't make America pre-eminent in science. When Sputnik went up, American prestige came down like a lead
balloon."

The Information officer dropped in while Tom was listing Delhi Post's assets. Tall and immaculate in a well-cut
bush shirt, Virgil Groom had a newsman's cynicism. "Don't
discount the competition," he growled. "They're swamp-
ing India with books, magazines, and pamphlets at prices
even paupers can pay. They're subsidizing the local Communist Party with the proceeds. They're spending folding
money to win the local press. They buy advertising space to
open editorial columns to their handouts. They commission
pieces from Indian journalists at better than going rates.
And if that doesn't get them what they want, they're ready
to supply cheap newsprint, a modern press, or a free trip
to Moscow and Peking. The Russians, Chinese, Poles,
Czechs, and all the others are busy out there"—Virgil
waved his arm in a gesture embracing all of India out-

side the capital—"handing the people a line that's hard
to beat. They say communism guarantees food, jobs,
schools, medicine. They say communism is a short cut to
progress."

Tom hitched his trousers and glanced at his watch.
"Say," he exploded, "it's time to eat. You're eligible for
membership in the Gourmet Society of Delhi Post. It is
dedicated to the propositions that no two Indian dishes
are created equal, and that no American can understand
India until he's sampled them all. Today is *tandoori* day at
Moti Mahal. Let me call the members and put your candi-
dacy to a vote."

The Gourmet Society was strictly stag. Perhaps its most
enthusiastic member was Jack Maddux, the Assistant Cultural Affairs Officer, a Falstaffian character of about thirty-
five with wide-ranging interests, not the least of which was
food. The Indians included Vic Kulanday, with a wide
white smile and the hushed, swift speech of a brooklet in
spate. Krishan Gujral had the prematurely gray hair and
prosperous paunch of a banker. Harbans Singh had the
beard and heft of a Sikh. Ali Hussein was a rugged Muslim
from Jammu. All were associated with Virgil in the press
section. On the cultural side was Ved Sethi, full of Yankee-
isms gathered during an American visit. Yash Gupta, his
side-kick, dark-skinned and dignified, had the high, me-
lodic voice of a *sitar*. Basil Monier, Delhi Post's administrative wizard, was of French descent, as round, sage, and
gentle as a Buddha. A non-meat-eating member who came
along for sociability's sake was Prem Verma, the Hindi
editor, a bald *sanyassi* with a Parker 51.

Moti Mahal was a Peshawari restaurant specializing in
chicken marinated in turmeric, cardamon, black pepper,
chili, and lime, and baked in a pit lined with Jumna river

mud. Of the many Muslim invaders crossing the North-west Frontier, only chicken *tandoori* had truly conquered India. Eaten with enormous flounder-shaped slabs of semi-leavened bread, it added an indispensable olfactory and gustatory dimension to the Indian experience.

The restaurant was busy. Fat gem dealers from Chandni Chowk, black-frocked barristers, Sikhs in turquoise tur-bans, their beards harnessed in hairnets, drifted in and out. When the door opened, the ululation of Hindi music from the Faiz bazaar overcame all conversation. When the door closed, Elvis Presley charged out of a juke box as chro-matic as the acacia, bauhinias, and flame-red gulmohars ushering in the neon brilliance of early summer. The first faint harbinger of the *loo,* the heat of the western desert that would soon incinerate the city, challenged one to stay and suffer, or to flee in the knowledge of having failed a test. I wanted to stay.

But memories of the morning shadowed my mood. The twisted image of America in Indian minds. The enormity of Delhi district. The pigmy proportions of Delhi Post's means. The sweep and scale of India's problems. Commu-nist cupidity. The marquee advertising the sexy American film. The sign: "Read Soviet Books." The collision in Con-naught Circus. The American: big, strong, swift, on the wrong side of the street. The Indian: "Someone should tell the sahibs to have a care!"

VI. Two Indias

Five mornings a week, at the crack of dawn, a *yogi* whispered outside my door. "Om! Om! Let us wake!" His name was Mr. Mukkerjee, a man of my own build, rather squat but incredibly supple. His face was serene, with the elliptical eyes and long-lobed ears of a Buddha. Stripped to a loin cloth, he would demonstrate the day's position. The bow: stomach on the floor, head and feet arched backward. Or the plough: head and shoulders on the mat, torso and legs swung over and back until toes touched the floor. Or the peacock: the body prone, levitated and balanced on forearms and wrists. Exercises like these, said Mr. Mukkerjee, were steps toward concentration, meditation, and the ultimate union of the individual personality with the Infinite.

Mr. Mukkerjee had been recommended by Ford Sessions, an attaché at the Embassy. Ford and I had met at a party shortly after my arrival in Delhi. Exhausted by a series of sixteen-hour days, I could hardly stay awake over my Scotch and soda. Ford smiled sympathetically. "If I were you," he said, "I'd take up *yoga*. Why not let me send my man Mukkerjee over in the morning?"

Ford explained that when he was too weary to face another official function, a massage by Mr. Mukkerjee pepped him up. On the other hand, when a rare evening came along without any social obligations, Mr. Mukkerjee manipulated a different set of nerves and muscles, inducing sleep. "Mukkerjee," Ford added, "is clean and speaks English. He can teach you not only the yogic postures but the philosophy as well. Once you've mastered *yoga*, Hinduism is an open book."

Next morning Mr. Mukkerjee led me to a grass mat spread on the verandah. Placing his feet a few inches apart, he drew his diaphragm into his rib cage, hollowing half the abdomen while the other half bulged like a tensed biceps. Then he reversed the action, tossing his knotted entrails like a basketball to the other side of his body. I strove to follow Mr. Mukkerjee's example. Unlike his stomach, divided into two parts, each independently activated, my own was a unitary object which I could compress slightly, but over which, otherwise, I had no control. While I grunted, Mr. Mukkerjee reached from behind, delivering a downward push in the area of the solar plexus. Breathless and almost lifeless, I collapsed. "Never mind," said Mr. Mukkerjee. "With a few years' practice it will be easy."

Ordering me to stretch out on the mat, Mr. Mukkerjee straddled my hips. "Will your day be busy?" he asked. I mumbled that it would. "Very well," he said, "I shall make you lively as Krishna chasing a milkmaid." His fingers danced over my body. My appreciation of the lightness of his touch was mitigated by a tendency to be ticklish. Each time he touched my armpits and thighs, I tensed.

Mr. Mukkerjee's voice was low and deep. "Close your eyes, sahib. Concentrate. Realize the Atman within you. Atman is the imperishable self." The yogi's fingers touched a nerve. I giggled, spoiling the solemnity of his revelation.

Eadie was waiting breakfast for me. I sat down, half asleep. She begged me to go back to bed, but my calendar forbade. I went to the office and yawned through an endless day.

The next evening was free of engagements. I told Mr. Mukkerjee I looked forward to eight hours of undisturbed sleep. The *yogi* gave me an understanding smile, kneaded me with heavy hands and talked of death. "Every act leaves its trace upon your Karma. Karma follows you like your shadow, from one existence to another. Though your body dies—please sahib, concentrate on my words and not on your underarms—the subtle body of Karma remains with the soul throughout all its rebirths. It disintegrates only with the soul's attainment of salvation."

That evening I headed for the bedroom and slipped between the sheets. But my mind and body tingled with the effects of Mr. Mukkerjee's massage. Not until dawn did I fall asleep, only to be awakened by the *yogi's* "Om!"

Yoga, clearly, was not for me. Whenever I had a free night for slumber, I paced the floor. At other times I almost had to be carried out, nodding, from official receptions. But Ford Sessions' words—"Once you've mastered *yoga*, Hinduism is an open book"—spurred me on. Besides, I was mystified by a trick of Mr. Mukkerjee. Prodding my abdomen in the morning, he would frequently comment on what I had eaten the night before. "*Moorg masalam,* chicken," he would say, fingering a coil of my intestine. "A *yogi* should not eat such pungent food." Or, after a bibulous night, "Liquors leave their mark on your Karma as well as on your liver."

Mr. Mukkerjee's ability to divine the original nature of the digested food within the internal organs defied my Western mind. Until, one morning, I overheard his words to the bearer as he climbed the steps to our rooms. "And last night," he asked, "what did sahib have for his supper?"

I teased Mr. Mukkerjee about having solved the mystery. "But sahib," he replied, "it was no mystery. I did not claim to know by supernatural means what you had eaten. I asked the bearer because it is the teacher's duty to know what his pupil eats and drinks. It is only the Western mind that makes a mystery of the East. Then, when it is disappointed, it charges the East with fraud."

Mr. Mukkerjee paused a moment. "Sahib," he said softly, "*yoga* is a path to self-realization. It is not an instrument of foreign policy. I wonder whether *yoga* is the path you should pursue."

Mr. Mukkerjee's words struck home. To embrace the fullness of Hindu philosophy would take a lifetime. All I had was fourteen days. A memorandum from Golf Links had come to my desk, notifying me of a meeting to be held at headquarters two weeks hence. The PAO's of all four Districts were asked to bring their plans for the new fiscal year. To formulate such plans I needed knowledge of Hinduism, Sikhism, and Islam sufficient to attune me to the thought processes of their practitioners. It was a tall order, impossible of fulfillment. But if plans proposed by Delhi Post were to hold prospects of success, some minimal understanding of the people seemed essential.

Mr. Mukkerjee and I parted with mutual relief. My Indian staff undertook my education. Prem Verma led me into Hindu temples. Harbans Singh opened the Sikh Gurudwara's gates, and read to me from the Holy Granth. Ali Hussein and I talked with Muslim *muftis* in tea stalls ringing the Jama Masjid, and attended *mushairas,* gatherings in obscure halls where Urdu poets recited revolutionary verse. One by one, steppingstones formed under my feet, leading toward understanding.

In a narrow lane, in a whitewashed house, a priest rang a bell and bowed in prayer. Women hovered over fertility symbols associated with conception and birth, festooning images of the male organ with marigolds. Men venerated plants, stones, and statues reputed to bring good weather, lush crops, and wealth. Idolatry was everywhere. In the confusion of paint-smeared genitalia and garish lithographs of legendary heroes and saints, I found few clues to the meaning of the Hindu faith.

The priest approached me with a toothless smile and talked about caste. "From the head of God sprang the scholar. From His arm emerged the soldier, brandishing a sword. From His thigh came the husbandman. From His feet came the servant. When a thorn entered the foot, the head bowed to remove it. The scholar served the servant, and vice versa. Each knew that it is upon its feet that mankind advances. Caste has been the savior of Indian society. It has fended off invaders. It has preserved our culture in defeat. Caste has made work honorable, spread employment, insured the families of the idle and the ill. Caste is the cement of our civilization. Destroy caste and you destroy India!"

The priest's son asked for a ride to Delhi. He was an intense young man who wore on his coat the hammer and sickle of ISCUS, the Indo-Soviet Cultural Society.

"It distresses me," he said, "to disagree with my father. Caste is incompatible with an industrial society. It flies in the face of all democratic thought, from Marx to Khrushchev. Reform is not the answer. Hinduism must go. Its practices are an affront to civilization. And the rest of the world must face up to deeper questions. Have not all traditional religions outlived their usefulness to mankind? Does religion belong in a technological age?"

I dropped him off at Delhi University. The Vice Chancellor was an old friend with whom I had once served on a UNESCO task force. He listened to my recital of the viewpoints of father and son and smiled. "When I went to America I was curious about Christianity. The answer depended on whom I asked. A single body of belief was interpreted in infinite ways. It led some Christians to abstinence and renunciation. It led others to acquisition and wealth. To some it meant preoccupation with the past. Among others Christianity whetted the thirst for knowledge that gave birth to the atomic age.

"And so it is with Hinduism. All levels of men are satisfied by this most tolerant of creeds. The intellectual can worship an abstract God and meditate on the meaning of reality. The artist can worship through music and dance. The primitive mind is comforted by myriad deities reincarnated in familiar objects, from the family's cook-pot to its sacred cow. All seek the same thing—the liberation of the spirit from the bondage of the body. Fanatics renounce earthly responsibility. But the thoughtful Hindu immerses himself in life, seeking fullest knowledge of its nature. To him, the hundreds of gods and goddesses in the Hindu pantheon come down to Brahman, the One Without Second. Whatever the outward difference between your faith and mine, we both acknowledge a single God."

The Vice Chancellor led me to the Great Hall of his College. Emblazoned on a wall were words in giant letters:

God is one. Wise men call Him by different names. May I be born again and again, in order to serve the poor, the downtrodden, the suffering. My God, the poor; my God, the wicked; my God, the miserable—the poor of all races and of all species, is the only God I worship.

"Hinduism means *dharma*," the Vice Chancellor said. "*Dharma* teaches that rights follow duties discharged. *Dharma* is the Hindu's defense against communism."

Eadie hired a nursemaid for Bret. He called her Kitty. A simple peasant woman, she added a deeper dimension to *dharma*. One day she brought her own youngest child to play with Bret. Suddenly a mad dog raced through the playground, lunging at the children with slathering jaws. Bret and her own boy were in the line of its charge, but too distant from each other to permit Kitty to protect both youngsters. Without hesitation, she picked up Bret. Later, Eadie asked her why she had not saved her own child who, fortunately, had escaped unhurt.

"It was God's duty to take care of my baby," Kitty answered. "It was my *dharma* to take care of Bret."

I found that the followers of India's ancient faiths were neither as exclusive as the West imagined, nor as hostile to infidels as history implied. The stranger who came in the spirit of search—without enmity, idle curiosity, conde-scension, or a camera—was welcome.

A *mufti* taught me that Islam meant peace, that Muslim meant submissive, and that the Prophet's teaching embraced the Judeo-Christian ethic. Harbans Singh explained that the word Sikh meant learner, and that the Sikh community was known as *khalsa,* meaning truth. I asked how such definitions could be reconciled with the post-independence partition riots when Muslims murdered Hindus, and Sikhs massacred Muslims. Rarely had the world seen such bloody civil strife.

The *mufti* shrugged. "Our faiths seek nonviolent solutions to mankind's problems. So does yours. But we are all mortal. Our actions do not match our ideals. Because we stumble and fall is no reason to put out the lamp that lights the way. All who believe in God must make the lamp burn that much more brightly."

Sitting in a Sikh temple, I was reminded of a New England town meeting. Resolutions were put before the entire congregation and vigorously debated. Then a vote was taken. The majority decision was binding on all. Of India's faiths, the Sikh community seemed the most democratic.

Yet into this deeply religious brotherhood communism had slipped a dagger's edge. A young Sikh named Gur-baksh Singh was sent to America to study. Returning home, he initiated a revival of Punjabi literature, modeling it after American writers of social protest and dissent. The movement attracted talented young Sikhs, and was insidi-ously captured by communism. Progressivism gave way to atheism. Once faith in God was breached, the movement became openly Communist, breaking the solidarity which for centuries had bound the Sikhs.

The black robe of the Supreme Court Justice set off the white halo of his hair. He considered my question: Could communism worm its way into the Hindu community as it had broken the solidarity of the Sikhs? He said that just as America inadvertently had contributed to communism's success in corrupting the Sikhs, so might America open Hindu minds to communism.

"It is your stubborn failure to understand the automatic reflex that colonialism implanted in every Hindu memory. This reflex tells us that the enemy of a white, Western nation may be India's best friend. Nothing helps communism so much as when an American presumes to instruct us about its evils. And nothing hurts America so much as your determination to base your case on purely American premises.

"It is not seemly for a jurist to teach a propagandist his trade. But if I, as a lawyer, had to plead America's case before an Indian jury, I would be careful to discuss democracy, free enterprise, military pacts, and other American policies in Indian terms. For instance, I would never argue for peace through collective security on the basis of American experience after World War II when you disarmed and suddenly found yourself faced by the Kremlin, alone and without arms. That simply makes you seem stupid. Rather, I would remind the jury that three thousand years ago India's villages pooled their men and arms to repel invasion. So long as these *samitis* dealt with enemies collectively, they kept India more or less at peace. Only when the common defense fell apart did India become vulnerable to Moghul invaders. And only through the failure of the Moghul princes to join in collective security measures did India succumb to the British."

The Justice gestured toward the books lining his chambers. "Torn from the pages of India's history, lessons like these have meaning for Indian minds. Your task is to relate America's aims to India's experience. When America asks Indians to defend themselves against communism for irrelevant reasons, it makes us more vulnerable to the very system it asks us to resist."

The editor rang the bell for the bearer and ordered tea for two. He asked to what he owed the pleasure of my visit. I said I had just joined USIS and was making the rounds of the Indian press. He said that meeting the Indian press was like going to a well and squeezing the dipper.

"If you want to drink, you must reach down in the well to the water. If you want to understand India, you must reach down to the people. Americans believe the way to approach the people is through the press. Perhaps a better way is to approach the press through the people. If you are genuinely interested in establishing better rapport between Americans and Indians, you will not operate as a press agent absorbed in getting his client's name in the daily papers. You will look beyond political situations to their roots, deep in the ethos of the masses."

I said the masses were many, and we Americans in USIS were few. In practical terms, we had to deal with the leaders of public opinion, and not with the led.

"You have come to the wrong person," the editor replied. "I am the led. The people are the leaders. You Americans err in your preoccupation with outstanding personalities. The more prosperous a man, the less he reflects the true conditions of his constituency. The more powerful a man, the more certain that he is primarily concerned with the perpetuation of his political power. Let your Ambassador deal with Mr. Nehru. That is his duty. Your own duty is to seek out the school teachers, the housewives, the carpenters, the clerks, and the illiterate multitudes who represent the real India. Make common cause with them and you need waste no time on me."

Not far from the Cecil Hotel was a village hardly different from any in the outback of India. The headman was careful not to harm the flies as he fanned them from his face. I asked him how information and ideas reached his village.

"In the same way," he said, "as news has always reached our village. Gandhiji taught us that little men must be their own newspapers. It is only men like ourselves that we can trust. If anything happens of interest to us, we can depend upon the blacksmith to hear of it as he shoes the horses. Whatever touches us—be it the price of cotton cloth in Allahabad or a shot fired by a Pakistani across our border —is soon grist for our gossip."

I asked the headman what he knew about America.

"America? Why should we know anything about America? What meaning has America for us?"

An author widely known in India and the West dropped by the office. We discussed my search for insights into his countrymen's minds. He said, "In 1835 a young man named Thomas Babington Macaulay became president of the Committee on Public Instruction. Be sure to read his 'Minute on Education' for colonial India."

The Minute concluded with these words:

It is impossible for us, with our limited means, to attempt to educate the body of the people. We must at present do our best to form a class who may be interpreters between us and the millions whom we govern; a class of persons, Indian in blood and color, but English in taste, in opinions, in morals and in intellect. To that class we may leave it to refine the vernacular dialects of the country, to enrich those dialects with terms of science borrowed from the western nomenclature, and to render them by degrees fit vehicles for conveying knowledge to the great mass of the population.

A few days later I received a letter from my friend. "In an independent India," he wrote, "nothing could be more fatal to yourselves, to us and to freedom than for you to strive to create a class of persons, Indian in blood and color, but American in taste, in opinion, in morals and intellect."

A group of us gathered in Mr. Nehru's office. The Prime Minister's urbanity masked the scars acquired in white men's prisons. But his words had the bite of a man who had forgotten nothing of his humiliation at Western hands.

Through socialism we are evolving an economy that appeals to the masses of our people, replacing the profit motive with cooperation. The acquisitive society which is at the base of capitalism has no future in India. Nor is there any future in India for ignorance. Science and technology represent the basic facts of life today. We cannot be untrue to them. But still less can we be untrue to those principles for which India has stood through the ages. The future will be empty if we ignore the wisdom of the past.

A captain escorted us from the Prime Minister's presence. In the Central Hall of Parliament he pointed to an inscription engraved on the wall:

Almighty God will not change the condition of any people unless they bring about a change themselves.

My eye was caught by the patch on the Captain's sleeve, the emblem of the Indian army. It was a sword, brandished by the arm of God.

Only a few days were left before the Public Affairs Officers' meeting. My knowledge of India remained insufficient to the need. But a sense of strangeness had given way to kinship. True, poverty, illiteracy, superstition, and all the ills of economic underdevelopment held India in their grip. In few places on earth, perhaps, did one see such debasement of human beings. Nowhere did ugliness so flagrantly assault and offend the senses—despite the temples and flowers that flourished amid the filth. And for all my efforts at understanding, many Indian ways of life remained so strange as seemingly to corroborate Kipling's edict that never the twain shall meet. But beneath the differences the congruity was great. India's ethical values, political principles, and social goals devolving from religious teaching were not unlike our own.

Evident too were other factors with vital bearing on my mission. First, in Indian minds, colonialism persisted as a major menace. Marxism was the enemy of colonialism, and therefore India's friend. No clumsy assertion of American viewpoints could cope with these convictions.

Second, while in Western societies cultural forms provided amusement or escape, centuries of suppression had fused the Indian people and their culture. To weaken or shatter their culture was to weaken or shatter the people. To reform or replace any aspect of it, even with the most benign intent, was a matter for caution and self-restraint.

Third, everyone above the age of twenty-one could vote and—despite the difficulties of reaching the polls, the inhibitive effect of illiteracy, the novelty of voting procedures—the Indian people were massively exerting their franchise in the greatest democratic elections on earth. This power was being exerted toward the achievement of what India deemed its legitimate aspirations for freedom, progress, and peace.

To Indians, freedom meant *moksha,* liberation of the soul from bodily bondage. National and individual sovereignty. The absence of colonial rule, the end of exploitation. The chance to be themselves, Indians, and not imitation Englishmen or Americans.

Progress meant enough to eat. A better chance for children. The alleviation of misery. Escape from "capitalist injustice." Progress meant industrialization on a massive scale, great dams, electrification and irrigation, the development of natural resources for the welfare of all, under the guidance of government.

Peace meant the discipline of the emotions, the body, and the mind, through meditation. An end to strife between rich and poor, through social justice. An easement of the inequalities caused by caste. Peace also meant Indian control of Kashmir and the headwaters of the Ganges. The restitution of property to Hindu refugees by Pakistan. The cessation of American military and economic aid to Pakistan. The expulsion of the Portuguese from Goa. The end, everywhere, of Western imperialism, of racism, of armaments, of atom bombs, of military pacts, of East-West truculence.

My search for understanding of the people of Delhi District revealed not one India, but two.

One was an India of Gold Flake cigarettes and pull-chain porcelain plumbing made by Shanks; of cricket, boiled mutton, blazers, and Oxford bags; of kilted Pathan bagpipers and Aldershot-type tattoos; of solar topees and sardine-savories; of Fabian Socialism and a cereal called Force; of Victorian architecture, high tea, and Thomas Babington Macaulay.

It was an India molded in the English image, aping English ways. To this India, Britain had bequeathed its language, its law, its educational system, its constitutional democracy, its parliamentarian skills, its civil service, its Western outlook, and ethic.

This India's English-speaking, English-trained elite was important. It made and executed Indian policy. It administered its laws and formulated its Five Year Plans. It ran India's railroads, post offices, and banks. It published its English language press and taught in its universities. Personified by its Prime Minister, Cambridge-educated, urbane, attuned to two worlds, its influence at mid-century in India and on the international stage was strong.

But this India rested on an eroding foundation. Thin, aging, increasingly alienated from indigenous inspiration, this remnant of English influence was passing away.

The other India was an India nourished by nationalism, struggling to free itself from alien influences, eager to be itself, to recapture its glory, to build a modern society upon a foundation of its own institutions.

This other India was being formed in schools, factories, farm cooperatives, labor unions, in lower echelons of provincial governments and political parties, in towns and villages outside the capital. Its attitudes and insights were Indian. Education was awakening the masses. Hindi was the official language of the land; regional dialects were displacing English. New impulses were welcomed from the outside world. But the acceptance of alien ideas depended on their compatibility with Indian value-judgments.

The villages of this other India were astir. Through democratic decentralization, authority and responsibility were being transferred from the central government to the councils of the people.

This other India was the India of the *Panchayat Raj,* an awakening of four hundred million farmers and workers whose grievances demanded redress, and whose will was decisive.

This other India, this Indian India, was gathering strength.

VII. The ides of March

Five days remained before the conference of Public Affairs Officers. An annual affair in which budget and other routine matters were tabled for discussion, the meeting held for a newcomer such as myself a sense of urgency. Events in March of 1958 posed problems for the U.S. Information Service all over the world. In India they were especially painful, clinching stereotypes about American capitalism, imperialism, and cultural barbarism.

The United States was scraping the bottom of the worst of the postwar slumps. Unemployment was at a seventeen-year high; production was at its lowest level since 1954. A Senate committee was uncovering "much that is shameful and unsavory" about the behavior of certain elements in American labor and management. Senators referred to "a hoodlum empire, the members of which are steeped in iniquity and dedicated to the proposition that no thug need starve if there is a Teamster payroll handy." All this was reported in the Indian press.

In foreign affairs, the United States seemed out of step

with Indian aspirations. Delhi papers hailed Soviet proposals for a foreign ministers' meeting as a preliminary to
a summit conference. Next day, they mourned America's
rejection of "the Soviet initiative toward peace." The USSR
struck another propaganda coup with the announcement
that it was halting atomic tests and with an invitation to
the United States to take similar action. The White House
termed the Soviet ban "a gimmick not to be taken seriously"—a position few Indians applauded. The Soviets
scored again with a proposal to establish a United Nations
agency to supervise outer space. Coupled with it was a
demand for liquidation of all overseas military bases.
United States officials correctly termed the offer "totally
unacceptable." But American obduracy was etched more
deeply in Indian minds.

Other items carrying a March dateline included a meeting of the South East Asia Treaty Organization in Manila.
Mr. Nehru's views on American collective security arrangements were no secret. Describing them as "a wrong approach, a dangerous approach, a harmful approach," he
condemned them for keeping up "the spirit of war and
violence that troubled the world." Pakistan's membership
in SEATO made the Manila meeting especially distasteful
to Indian opinion. Even American successes that month
had a jingo ring. The U.S. Navy announced the launching
of the first Vanguard satellite, and the smashing of trans-
Atlantic undersea records by its atomic submarine, the
Skate. The U.S. Army put Explorer III into earth-circling
orbit. While boosting the stock of American science, these
triumphs cemented the belief that "capitalist progress"
was geared more to war than to peaceful purposes.

Against these tidings I weighed Golf Links' invitation
to present our plans. The situation seemed to demand

more than a routine response to budget and other house-keeping problems. A great democracy, acting openly, was generating a flow of news that sharpened India's anti-American prejudices. Our task was to submit evidence enabling Indians to judge events in some truer perspective. The seeming insuperability of the task was the measure of the challenge we confronted. I looked forward to the PAO meeting, to the interchange of experience, the clash of ideas which alone could assure an adequate answer to the Communist challenge. I resolved to be as responsive to Golf Links' request for ideas as circumstances allowed. Relying on the advice of my staff as well as on my own impressions of India, I hoped to present a sensible précis of Delhi Post's plans.

In the little time remaining before the meeting, I examined the current USIS operation. Jane Williams placed before me position papers prepared by Golf Links, citing the USIS mission in India, defining its audience, and describing the projects designed to achieve its objectives.

Our mission, it appeared, was to present evidence that the United States was qualified, militarily, economically, culturally, and intellectually, to lead the nations of the free world, and to serve as their spokesman.

Our audience was a small elite: government officials, university presidents, students, and leaders of communication media.

As for USIS projects, they numbered over fifty. Some were locally conceived and produced. Others utilized materials supplied by the Agency from Washington. Reliance rested mainly on the printed word, with the *American Reporter* the keystone of a sizable publications program.

I was face to face, I realized, with the classic conflict that underlay my mental reservation about the Agency:

a conflict concerning the Agency's mission, audience and method; a conflict between the Agency and its detractors that had never been resolved.

Admittedly, Golf Links' approach was beguiling. The most oppressive feeling an American faced in a country such as India was a sense of his own inadequacy amid overwhelming odds. Delhi District alone had 338,180 villages. For one American to visit them all would take many lifetimes. The country was too big, the people too many, the problems too complex, the barriers too high to permit communication with the general public. Besides, how much did the general public really matter? Might not the ideal of mass communication with peoples, and not just elites, rest on purely American conjectures? How genuinely democratic was the Indian personality? In Arthur Koestler's words, "How could a citizen be expected to elect a government when he was not allowed to elect his own bride?"

Answers to questions such as these substantiated Golf Links' estimate of the situation. On the other hand, Golf Links' approach seemed to reflect the very ills so often cited by the Agency's critics.

Its concept of mission seemed insensitive to Indian psychology. Indian independence was eleven years old. The taste of freedom was sweet. To direct their own destiny, to make their own voice heard, to avoid becoming an echo of others were the deepest desires of this newly sovereign people. Having thrown off British leadership, Indians hardly seemed likely to accept a satellite relationship with another Western power. It was as if, after the Revolutionary War, some European country had proclaimed its qualifications to lead and speak for the United States.

I recognized America's unique position in the world. I

was aware that leadership had been thrust upon us. But such leadership had been conferred, not usurped. For America to advertise its supremacy cast doubt upon its claims, and vitiated the relationship between the leader and the led.

More important, the United States stood for self-determination, equality, national sovereignty: the right of every people to determine its own destiny, uncoerced by others. Communism sought to impose its leadership on the world, with the Kremlin speaking for the whole human race. Golf Links' aim—the affirmation of America's right to lead, of India's fate to follow—represented a reversal of these two diametrically opposite positions. For the Kremlin to emerge as the champion of Indian sovereignty seemed grotesque.

Golf Links' position on audience also seemed open to question. Like Thomas Babington Macaulay in his "Minute on Education," USIS-India seemed to assume that assiduous cultivation of sophisticated Indians could make them Americans "in taste, in opinions, in morals and intellect." In an independent India, such an assumption seemed illusory. It virtually guaranteed the formulation of a message addressed toward the prosperous, satisfied upper class, solidifying the stereotype we were so anxious to expunge: that Americans were hungry for power, aloof from the miseries of the masses, bereft of the humanity on which our democratic pretensions were based.

As for the diffusion of USIS's limited resources over such a panoply of projects, here too I sensed a contradiction of the President's intent: to disregard the trivial, concentrating instead on those aspects of United States life that facilitated understanding of our objectives and were relevant to India's aspirations.

Oddly, Golf Links' policies had not been established without access to facts. Indeed, considerable money and effort were being spent on assessments of Communist activity. An exhibit of 168 Communist publications had been amassed, together with other evidence of Soviet efforts to woo the humblest Indian voter. Golf Links certainly understood the broad basis of popular consent on which the Indian government rested. It fully appreciated the degree of popular discontent that presaged change. Nor were the pace and power of elementary education in vernacular languages overlooked; the bulk of USIS output was in Hindi and other regional tongues.

But somehow, Golf Links' activities didn't square with the results of its own research. Preoccupation with a tiny elite minority hardly reflected the degree to which the Indian masses were exercising their franchise. It took little knowledge of that minority to measure how distant it was from the people, or how vain was the hope that India's accredited leaders would "decode" an alien message and disseminate it among their constituencies. Our publications were hardly on a par with those displayed in Golf Links' exhibit of Communist magazines. Packed with Americana, they reflected far more self-consciousness than sensitivity to Indian attitudes, and lacked the Communist's earthy people-to-people touch. As for our vernacular publications, their content was largely a literal translation of American materials, with few concessions to local idioms or tastes.

My own misgivings about the USIS program in India were supported, in the main, by the experience of my staff. I was especially attentive to the judgment of my Indian associates, who knew best the reactions of their countrymen to American propaganda. Many had been with USIS for over a decade. Invited to speak, they were hesitant at first to voice their thoughts. Gradually, however, they responded to the spirit of objective inquiry that characterized our sessions.

Over the years, the staff agreed, USIS had exerted a positive influence on Indo-American relations. Personal dealings between USIS officers and India's upper classes were cordial. A considerable amount of USIS material was being placed in the metropolitan press. A "college-contact" program aimed at bringing the higher aspects of American culture to faculties and students of major institutions. Helen Semmerling, my predecessor, had personally visited many communities that had hitherto never seen an American woman. On the whole, a distinct improvement in Indo-American amity was noted at official levels. For this, credit was given to a long list of happy ambassadorial choices, from Loy Henderson to Ellsworth Bunker, the incumbent, whose dignity and sincerity endeared him to the Indians among whom he worked. Good words were also spoken of their wives; Harriet Bunker magnificently represented all that was gracious in American womanhood.

The Ambassador's public activities ranged from major addresses to flag raisings, ribbon cuttings, and baby bouncings. All involved planning, coordination, and follow-through by USIS. Other Americans—Embassy officials, Consuls-General, PAO's and VIP's—all required and received the same attention. Simply dealing with the daily news—"fighting headlines," as the staff put it—was a yeoman's task. No one, perhaps, put the problem better than the Country Information Officer. "Our biggest headaches always seem to arise from statements, policies, and events that need explanation, refutation, or exploitation as they ebb and flow in the local media." None of this, the

staff felt, should be discounted in totting up the considerable total of USIS success.

It was of USIS failures, however, that the staff spoke
with deepest feeling. Listening to their critique of USIS
performance was like hearing a playback of our actions
in China prior to the Communist take-over. I wondered
how often the errors would have to be repeated before the
lessons sank in. USIS aimed at the pinnacle of India's
population; communism burrowed at the base, driving
toward farmers, workers, minor government officials, and
educated malcontents. While we dealt with those presently in power, communism aimed at the successors to the
present regime. USIS cultivated presidents of major universities. Communists infiltrated the faculties. USIS sought
out the owners and editors of principal newspapers; Communists operated at the levels of subeditors, leader writers,
reporters, printers, engravers, and delivery boys. USIS concentrated on so-called "opinion molders"; so did communism, but its eyes rarely left the voters—the innumerable,
anonymous masses of India in whose hands, ultimately,
lay the destiny of Indian democracy. USIS busied itself
with what someone called "infighting." It dealt with daily
news and, lacking an enduring philosophy, reacted to special situations. Communists followed a long-range strategy
toward constant goals, endlessly dinning into the people's
ears the same slogans: peace, jobs, food, freedom.

American cultural activity in India was criticized as
being on too high a plane. I had already sampled its rather
rarified quality. A troupe of players from a Western university had arrived in New Delhi earlier in the month. For
five nights running, at Sapru House, the capital's Carnegie
Hall, they had performed the tragedies of Eugene O'Neill.
The caliber of their stagecraft was superb, but the plays

dwelt unrelievedly on the dreary aspects of American life so skillfully dramatized by O'Neill. The theater was only half full, with the foreign and American diplomatic set more in evidence than the Indian public.

Each evening, however, a young Indian woman had occupied the seat beside mine. I complimented her on her enthusiasm for serious drama. Introducing herself as a Golf Links employee, she said her attendance was in the line of duty. She added that she didn't enjoy O'Neill at all. Indeed, she had gone backstage to ask the actors why they didn't mix some lighter fare with the tragic. The manager of the troupe had explained, "We were warned in Washington that Indians didn't like to laugh."

"Nothing," said the young woman, "could be farther from the truth."

Gradually, through the eyes of my Indian staff, I discerned the distorted pattern of our propaganda. The process was not easy. Introspection comes naturally to Indians; but as one confided to me, "Criticism is another matter. We are hired to do our jobs and keep our mouths quiet. Speaking so frankly makes us afraid of hurting somebody's feelings." When I assured the staff that no American official's feelings could possibly be hurt by constructive criticism, they went on to single out other areas of weakness the coming PAO conference might profitably consider.

The handling of American aid to India was of special concern. Expenditures on economic and technical assistance neared two billion dollars. Yet few things antagonized Indians as much as being reminded of American largesse. USIS had not evolved a method of dealing with this problem. It tended to go along with the Indian government's desire to emphasize agreements signed rather than to associate America with visible results benefiting the Indian people. Farm fairs, cattle shows, cooperative organizations, Community Development centers, labor unions rarely saw a USIS officer. Our Technical Cooperation Mission operated at one pole. USIS activity occurred at another.

The concentration of activity in New Delhi drew fire. True, USIS personnel frequently visited sites of colleges and other important institutions. But few of the fifty cities in the District with populations over 20,000 were favored with regular appearances of several days' duration during which USIS delved beneath the upper crust. As for the villages, "in the USIS scheme of things," in one staffer's words, "they don't exist. There's no substitute for a real flesh-and-blood American going out and getting to know the people. Instead, we're buried under paper work, reports, red tape."

USIS resources, some staffers felt, were being splintered by too many peripheral projects. Only rarely were money and manpower concentrated behind a single theme. Films, pamphlets, exhibits, radio, press output—each pursued solitary paths of inspiration.

In the enormous quantity of materials flowing into India from Washington, the staff opined, there was much of value. Special features, photo packets, magazine reprints, byliners, and the like provided a solid foundation for many a piece of India-angled copy. But the bulk of Agency output was said to be so excessively American-centered as to be virtually valueless in India. Too much of it stressed divisive factors, such as America's higher living standards, or accented the frivolous aspects of American life. A science feature recently received from the Agency's press branch in Washington was offered in evidence. Headlined "Bananas Have Nerves," the item revealed the results of

American scientific inquiry into the anatomy of the banana. It had all the man-bites-dog appeal by which American journalism judged a good story. Like editors everywhere, Indians had a weakness for the bizarre. The piece had enjoyed a big play. Such trivia accounted for a large percentage of USIS placements in the Indian press. On hard core items dealing with difficulties such as those the United States was experiencing during the current month, the harvest of clippings was sparse.

Two evenings were given over to a critique of USIS films. Ved Sethi picked from the catalogue of almost a thousand titles those with greatest relevance to India. All told, about thirty subjects were screened for our inspection. To broaden audience reaction, we invited our wives and included a leavening of illiterates: sweepers, bearers, and drivers employed by the office.

The consensus was that the films fell short of their potential. By rough estimate, an audience would have needed about twenty hours of consecutive viewing time to comprehend, fragmentarily, our policies on peace. But rarely did any audience attend more than an hour or so of USIS screenings in a year. The reasons were obvious: an enormous population, vast distances, our limited means.

We watched the films on peace without the sound track, an exercise suggested to approximate their impact on non-American or illiterate audiences. The visual image often delivered a message exactly opposite to the one intended. Scenes of troop demobilization, of movements of men and arms, of battlefields, death, and destruction were intended to depict our hatred of war. Observed without understandable explanation, they often suggested a pathological glorification of military power.

Several films dealt with the United States economy.

None grappled with the prejudices implanted by Marxist arguments. Almost all painfully accented the disparity between American abundance and Asian poverty. The lessons of American productivity remained unrelated to non-American situations.

The other films we saw suffered from the same non-awareness of audience. None dealt with mutual aid in an Asian frame of reference. Issues central to the idealogical conflict raging all over the world—the individual's right to think, to speak, to pray—were presented in an American idiom, incomprehensible to an average Indian. Only one film, an acquisition from Pan American Airways, hinted at the vigor and variety of the American scene.

Underlying the inadequacies of United States propaganda, the staff tended to agree, were three factors. One was a lack of long-range planning directed toward the specific problems the United States faced in India. The greater part of American effort was being expended on day-to-day news, and on cultural activities irrelevant to Indian needs and interest. The flood of "bad news" from America could neither be stemmed at the source nor diluted at the destination. The only way to deal with it was to supply Indians with some sane basis for judging the nature of American society. To do this were needed superb films, features, publications and exhibits, employing all the genius the Agency could command.

A second factor was an absence of empathy. Projecting American ideals and desires in India simply hardened the image of an America unwilling to comprehend another culture, demanding that others adjust their values to its own, indulging in the old imperial fantasy of its own superiority.

A third factor dealt with the real nature of the Communist threat in India. India was in the early stages of a gigantic upheaval. The masses were groping toward a new day. The Communist Party of India was identifying itself with the past and future of these people, posing as the prophet of a better life. Its motto: "Communism means guaranteed employment" had potent appeal to the jobless and hungry. USIS was failing to match communism's ideological power. Indian staffers, paradoxically, saw certain disadvantages in the Communist position. The Communist Party of India was tarred with the Moscow-Peking brush, whereas USIS had, in India's own political, social, and cultural institutions, unparalleled scope for intelligent action. In the traditions and hopes of the common people, in the glory of India's past and in its hopes for the future, lay democracy's strength. America needed only to understand and associate itself with these indigenous impulses.

Little time was left to hammer out Delhi Post's proposals. I asked the staff how they felt about undertaking an experiment in communication between the peoples of India and the United States, sticking literally to the letter and spirit of the President's mandate. Without exception, the staff endorsed the idea. Working through the last week end before the PAO conference convened, we prepared a paper.

It began with the President's statement of our mission. It urged examination of its emphasis on indigenously oriented programming. The paper then cited a recent report of the United States Advisory Commission on Information, stressing "the urgent need for long-range planning in the international communications field." We recommended that Golf Links define its themes for the ensuing year on which it desired Agency support, and that it advise Washington of the exact actions it desired the Agency to take. We added rough scripts for films on peace, aid, communism, and the American way of life, written with an eye on all Asia.

The paper admitted the impossibility of a handful of Americans and Indians in Delhi Post communicating directly with the 110 million people in the District. Nevertheless it established the general public as the audience of the American message. It designated as "decoders"—the elements in Indian society through whom the American message must move to the masses—the 15 per cent of the people who were quasi-literate in English or vernacular languages.

To reach this 15 per cent, numbering approximately sixteen million souls, Delhi Post proposed several measures. First, the formulation of an American message that had meaning to the masses. Second, the conversion of this message into pictures and simple language the people could comprehend. Third, the movement of the message as close as possible to the masses—specifically, to every city in the District with a population over 20,000, and to every town with a newspaper, school, or other instrument through which the communication process could be expanded. Fourth, the regularization of visits, with a minimum of one visit per city a year.

The paper urged reliance on Indian rather than on American publications. It proposed a reduction of time spent by Americans in their offices, and an expansion of time spent meeting people in the field. It accented excellence: the investment of money and effort in fewer activities, better done. It stressed the spirit of service. While the basic task of USIS must be to place the United States in correct perspective, it should seek to assist Indian development in the process.

Such were our purposes. That the goal far exceeded our resources we were aware. That few of us had experience in dealing with people below elite levels was acknowledged. That travel into the remote corners of the District invited risks—this too was accepted. No vast or costly undertaking was envisaged. The idea, rather, was to make a beginning, to probe toward the heart of the Indian people, to try to synchronize America's heartbeat with theirs.

Jane Williams pulled the last page from the mimeo machine late in the night preceding the PAO meeting. Virgil Groom hopped into the office jeep and delivered a dozen copies to Golf Links. Exhausted, I descended the stairs to the darkness of the street. My friend the fortune teller tugged at my sleeve. "Please sahib, you are a *neem* leaf, tossed about by the breeze. Please, sahib, let me bring you melted butter."

I threw him an anna and went home to bed. I didn't want melted butter. What I wanted was that Golf Links bless our proposals with its understanding and consent.

VIII. Golf Links

In the heart of the fashionable section housing New Delhi's foreign colony spread a green expanse of forest and fairway. Dotting the lawns were the Lodi tombs, relics of the sixth of the seven civilizations built upon the Jumna plain. Afghan in style, they were the legacy of Sher Shah Suri, who conquered northern India in 1539. Now "Fore!" echoed under the domes, and balls bounced off the mossy walls, sometimes retrieved by monkeys taunting the players from the trees. Not far from a trap near the twelfth hole stood a two-story residence converted into offices. Above it flew the United States flag. On the garden gate a small sign read United States Information Service. This was the home of USIS-India, known as Golf Links.

The pretty telephone operator in the foyer waved me into the conference room. Greeting the incoming Branch PAO's was the Country Public Affairs Officer, a broad-shouldered man in his early fifties. A homespun simplicity suggested his Midwestern beginnings, and a meticulous-

ness of speech pointed to pedagogy as his original profession.

His Deputy, short and robust, was a man of long experience as a missionary in India before his USIS days. He
was on intimate terms with many of India's leading politicians, and had written extensively on Gandhi, whom he
had known at Sevagram. Beside him stood the Country
Information Officer, an experienced newspaperman, his
grin as affable as his handshake, and the Country Cultural
Affairs Officer, a white-haired, courtly former dean of an
eastern university.

Sitting around the long table were my colleagues from
the other Branch Posts. The Bombay PAO had been a
professor of journalism. The Madras PAO, impeccably at-
tired in raw silk, had left a career in broadcasting to join
the Foreign Service. The Calcutta PAO had supervised
secondary schools in India and Burma between the two
world wars. His white linen suit matched the tendrils
tufting his head and accented the pinkness of his skin.
Folding chairs lined the walls, occupied by chiefs of radio,
exhibits, publications, and other headquarters sections.

The group represented a complement of over seventy
United States officers in India, forty at headquarters, the
others divided among the four Branch Posts. Germany ex-
cepted, it was the biggest USIS organization in the world.
Certainly no other country warranted a greater array of
talent. The people present seemed well equipped to meet
India's challenge. They were drawn from many of the professions for which America was famed: education, journalism, advertising, radio. Even the social sciences had a
spokesman in the person of a Research Officer with a doc-
torate degree. Though salaries were sizable in a country
where per capita incomes averaged under sixty dollars a

year, they were reasonable by American standards. Base pay of the Country PAO was $16,060; of the Branch PAO's, $13,640. Including housing, cost of living and hardship allowances, the nine senior officers around the table represented a payroll of about $150,000—a sum that seemed sufficient to buy the competent counsel and services the United States deserved.

Two late arrivals squeezed into the room, and promptly at nine o'clock the conference convened. The newcomers were introduced as "anxiously awaited visitors from the Agency, bearing tidings from the Great White Father in Washington." Laughter rumbled around the table. The smaller of the visitors was an owlish young man, representing the Chief of the Agency's Central Asia division. The other supervised low-cost book production overseas. The Country PAO explained that the date of the conference had been set to take advantage of the presence of the Washington guests, and turned the meeting over to the man from the Central Asia office.

I poised pencil over paper to take down the gist of his remarks. Whatever they might be, the morning's news had supplied an ominous prelude. From Lebanon, keystone in the arch of levantine states fringing the eastern Mediterranean, had come the first whisper of impending war. The pro-Western policies of President Camille Chamoun were under attack by pro-United Arab Republicans, Druse tribesmen, and Syrian arms smugglers. Nasser's fleet was being beefed up with Communist submarines, and Soviet TU 104's were arriving at Cairo's airport. An air of crisis was building up in Asia. The United States might soon find itself on another hot spot. Whether Washington used force to save Lebanese independence or permitted another free nation to drift down the drain—either way the repercussions in India would be strong.

Nor was Lebanon the only cloud on the horizon of Indo-United States relations. Less foreboding, but threatening a nasty squall, was the imminent arrival in India of Paul Robeson, the American Negro artist. A movement was gaining ground to make his birthday a national celebration, with India offering homage to a great singer of spirituals, a champion of the underdog, a credit to his race. Of Robeson's Communist affiliations and disloyalty to the United States India seemed to know little and to care less. A tempest was in the making, with USIS in the middle. I mentally blessed the Agency for its prescience in sending someone to brief us on Washington policy at so portentous a time.

The visitor's voice was as quiet as his appearance. He said that a Career Legislation Bill had been introduced before Congress. It sought to provide the Foreign Service corps of the Information Agency the same rights guaranteed to the Department of State. Tenure, pensions, and other privileges denied to Agency personnel were being requested. Anticipating passage of the bill, the Agency was instituting a series of examinations. Those who passed would become career officers entitled to the benefits envisaged by the bill.

The news was greeted with delight. Only the nature of the examination caused concern. All the Washington visitor could say was that it doubtless would be fair. The Country PAO expressed the hope that knowledge of a foreign language would not be a requirement for the Career Service. He felt Congress and the Agency were unrealistic in their emphasis on language competence; senior officers were too busy to give time to the study of exotic vernaculars.

The visitor went on to explain a new policy relative to duty tours of Agency personnel. Henceforth, he said, officers would sandwich two years of domestic duty between every four years of service overseas, rather than proceed from one foreign assignment to another. This drew a mixed response, with the majority showing little enthusiasm for work in Washington.

The visitor came to the climax of his mission. From the Director down, he said, everyone in the Agency had done a bang-up job preparing for the annual budget hearings. Months had been devoted to culling world-wide evidence of program effectiveness. As a result, there was room for hope that Congress would increase the Agency's allowance for the coming year. India was of crucial importance. If Golf Links presented a good case for funds to meet its special needs, he felt sure the Agency would give it sympathetic attention.

The Deputy glanced at the wall clock and suggested that no time be lost in getting down to an assessment of USIS-India's needs. He solicited suggestions from the Branch PAO's. One asked for funds to construct an animated electric "ticker tape" around the building in which the USIS offices were located. Overlooking a main thoroughfare, it would flash news to the crowds like the revolving sign in New York's Times Square. Another officer proposed a plan to install hi-fi equipment in the colleges and universities of his District, and to circulate packets of American jazz records. "The syllogism is obvious. I like jazz. Jazz is American. Therefore I like America." A third PAO urged a campaign to publicize American aid to India. He felt that existing low-key aid programs were not getting across.

The Country Information Officer said that Indians were fed up with publicity on American aid. USIS should spend its money on more useful projects, such as calendars. He held up the current year's specimen. Illustrating each of the twelve months was a full-color scene of Americans at work or play. Each page advertised "United States Information Service."

Calendars, said the Country Information Officer, had proved their value time and again. In evidence, he recounted a story told to him by a well-known newsman who had gone down to Kerala to interview the head of the Communist Party. When the newsman entered the functionary's office, he was astonished to see a USIS calendar on the wall. "How effective is it for our program?" the Information Officer asked. "One never knows, but at least the exposure is there, and it is not too far-fetched to believe that at some time the idea of American interest and friendship may percolate down in a positive, friendly form."

The remainder of the morning was devoted to a discussion of how next year's calendar might improve on the current version. American industry was chosen as the theme. It was agreed that the Agency should be asked to supply color photographs on this subject. The Country PAO approved the budgeting of funds for one hundred thousand calendars of this costly type, plus ten thousand simpler single-page affairs to be given away to a lower order of recipients.

Lunch intervened. I had little appetite. Like most newcomers, I was suffering a bout of illness known locally as

"Delhi Belly." My malaise was aggravated by a presentiment that something was seriously wrong.

For the remainder of the day attention focused on the *American Reporter*. This fortnightly tabloid newspaper took the biggest bite out of the USIS budget. Published in English and six regional languages, the *Reporter* was the heaviest gun in the American arsenal in India. Arrayed against it was a powerful battery of Communist publications. The USSR produced *Soviet Land* and *Soviet Woman*. Communist China circulated *China Pictorial* and *China Reconstructs*. North Korea, Poland, other satellites were also represented by first-rate magazines. Between full-color covers were packed articles about the attractiveness of life for the peasants, workers, and intellectuals in Communist lands. India was flattered with numerous articles respectful of its people and culture. Concern for humbler folk, for women, infants, youth, and for the colored races stamped almost every page. Handsomely illustrated, and printed on paper of good quality, they clearly outclassed the *American Reporter*.

Branch PAO's pointed out the disparity with passion. The *Reporter* was said to be neither a newspaper nor a magazine. It was over the heads of ordinary Indians, yet too crudely propagandistic for sophisticated tastes. Its news was history by the time the fortnightly came off the press. Many of its features were Washington-manufactured "boiler plate," irrelevant to India. Printed on cheap pulp, its illustrations were "muddy," its style "dull as ditch water." USIS should publish either a first-class magazine or a daily newspaper in the best American tradition.

The PAO's' criticisms were corroborated by Golf Links' Research Officer. A scholarly-looking man with rimless glasses, he read excerpts from a survey of 3,322 Indian readers of the *Reporter's* English language edition. Its gist was that on every count—readability, interest, empathy—the *Reporter* ran second to Communist publications. It was doing little to uphold American prestige. Indeed, many Indians frankly stated that the tabloid fell short of what they expected of an American publication.

The Country PAO, with an anxious glance at the clock, signaled a halt to the discussion. He said he saw no cheaper way of reaching so large an audience with the American story. It was foolhardy, he felt, to condemn a publication that had endured so long, despite its critics. We shouldn't forget that when the tide of Indian opinion was adverse, and Indian editors refused to print the American position, the *Reporter* could be counted on to carry the freight. Branch PAO's were invited to state their requirements without further delay, so that everyone could wash up and get ready for the evening's session. The result was a planned increase in existing editions up to 200 per cent. Two editions would be added, one in Kannada and one in Gujerati.

We gathered at the Country PAO's home for cocktails and a buffet dinner. Shop talk held sway, centering principally on the prospects of Agency personnel acquiring career status. The party broke up early but I could not sleep.

Next morning, the chiefs of Golf Links' various sections put forward their budget requests for the coming year. Asserting the effectiveness of current undertakings, they hinted of even better things to come. The Publications Officer passed around for approval a booklet dealing with the impending Lincoln Sesquicentennial. Facing each other, page after page, were almost identical pen portraits of Lincoln and Gandhi, with a few excerpts of their remarks on democracy and freedom. The Exhibit Officer's plans also dwelt on this theme. He presented a poster featuring portraits of the two leaders, plus a package of photographs to be arranged as a display. Other media chiefs requested additional funds, principally to expand current activities in radio and the press, or to replace worn-out items, such as books in libraries. On films, the decision was to ask the Agency to produce a picture depicting India's progress. The Agency would also be asked to increase the number of reels available for distribution in India, without regard to theme.

The low-cost book program led to a lengthy exchange between the second visitor from Washington and Golf Links officers. I was too new to the business to understand the intricacies of the book-translation operation. Apparently books were being printed and bound in Bombay and then delivered to junkmen who converted them into paper bags for wrapping vegetables in the bazaars. Despite the muddle, a considerable increase in the book program was planned. Titles of books suitable to the Indian market were not specified.

On the cultural side, discussion centered on the value of seminars and visiting lecturers. Agreement was reached on three points which the Deputy duly noted in the minutes of the meeting. One, the utility of seminars depended on the abilities of the participants. Two, the success of touring lecturers depended on their ability and adaptability. Three, visiting lecturers needed to be better briefed on the conditions they would encounter in India.

India drifted farther and farther away. The Coca Cola bottles, the paper cups, the Palm Beach ties, the smell of Lucky Strikes, the division of dollars—all seemed remote from reality. Even the India visible through the venetian blinds was a country of putting greens, fairways, and sand traps. My own contribution to the meeting had been nil. Copies of the paper Delhi Post had prepared had been placed on the table. But as the second day waned, I realized the ideas it espoused were unread and unconsidered. I asked permission to speak and the Country PAO nodded.

I said I was confused by the conference. It failed to make clear the rationale of the USIS program. Jazz and electric signs didn't seem adequate answers to the problems we faced in India. Granting that calendars were fine for advertising hair tonics and soft drinks, their usefulness in harmonizing Indian and American aspirations seemed open to question. I, for one, had little hope that a calendar could convert the head of Kerala's Communist Party.

The decision on the *American Reporter* struck me as strange, in view of the publication's admitted inferiority. To change its format, to experiment with its content and style—these seemed more reasonable than to increase the circulation of the present product. Nor could I comprehend the allotment of more funds to low-cost books before clearing up doubts about the fate of existing editions. What, incidentally, was the determinant of an effective book program in India: the expenditure of funds, or the careful selection of titles suitable to India's needs?

I touched on films. Why was the Agency not given guidance on the few films we so urgently needed? Perhaps, if we suggested worthwhile themes, the Agency might put our problem before the most talented people in the motion picture industry. Hollywood had genius, money, the will to serve America. What it didn't have was the Agency's experience in communicating with unsophisticated audiences, some of whom had never seen a motion picture, and almost all of whom believed the image of America Hollywood portrayed. Properly advised, Hollywood might produce superior films that leaped over barriers of background and language.

As for the conference's conclusions on the cultural program, did these represent an intelligent response to the magnitude of Indian prejudice? Indians believed our culture to be debased, our women and children debauched, our economy exploitive, our God mammon. Did this meeting have no better solution to suggest than that "the utility of a seminar depends on the abilities of its participants"?

I asked that the Indian people be considered in our deliberations. They were important. The importance of people was the basic tenet that gave America birth and made it great. If America meant anything at all, it was that the individual, however humble, was precious and entitled to determine his own destiny. In India, as in America, the people would determine their own destiny.

These people were many, and we were few. Only a message conceived with their interests in mind might pave its own path to the towns and villages where they lived. Dollars couldn't break down the barriers of ignorance that divided our peoples. Propaganda couldn't convert anyone to freedom's cause. Communication with the Indian people depended on our knowledge of their culture, on our response to their problems, and on our will to meet with them on a basis of mutual respect.

These sentiments seemed to strike a chord in the Branch PAO's. One of them described a USIS exhibit at a *mela* or country fair. Thousands of farmers had flocked to see it. This rare example of American interest in them and their problems had made a deep impression.

Another Branch PAO added that the peasants were on the move. The Government of India was serious about its Community Development plans. The entire point and purpose of American aid was to galvanize the villages. USIS had an obligation, and an opportunity, in this area. It was high time we did something about it.

The Golf Links side of the table was cool. The Country Information Officer said that we were raising an old question: Should we plan our program and freeze it into a rigid pattern? Or was it better to adapt to situations as they arose? Old-timers long ago had learned the answer. The only way to operate was to keep flexible. It made no sense to set up a basic program and follow it through no matter what the immediate news might be. As a man with news and media training, he could only reject such a philosophy.

The Deputy added that twenty-five years in India had made him dubious about trying to reach the Indian people. Even were it possible, he doubted the value of the results. The people played a passive role. The upper class held the power of decision. As for the Community Development program, it was a noble idea but despite all the Government's efforts, the villages were stagnant. For USIS to waste time and money on them would distract it from its main job: the cultivation of India's elites.

A sentence from E. M. Forster's *A Passage to India* flashed across my mind. "I have had twenty-five years' experience of this country," he paused, "and twenty-five years seemed to fill the waiting room with their staleness and ungenerosity."

The entrance of the Ambassador ended the discussion. Gracious and poised, he eased his long frame into a chair. Then gravely, in a voice hardly higher than a whisper, he briefed us on the situation as he saw it. On the whole, he sensed betterment in Indo-American relationships over the past few years. In the Indian mind, however, colonialism remained a far greater threat than communism. India should not be judged by a Western yardstick. Unless a man had lived under colonial rule, he could have no idea of what it did to the mind and spirit. Confident that time was on its side, the Communist Party of India was waiting until Nehru was out of the way to unleash its power. USIS must remember this in its own operations.

The task of USIS was as difficult as it was important. Arms aid to Pakistan fed the myth of United States militarism. We needed to bring the most impressive talent of the United States to convince Indians that our policies were directed toward peace. He wondered whether one such man as Muñoz Marin might not do more good, by relating the accomplishments of "Operation Bootstrap" in Puerto Rico to the problems of India, than expensive cultural efforts aimed over the average Indian's head.

The arrival of Paul Robeson, he warned, would embarrass us. He hoped our conference was readying plans. He advised against our entering into public controversy on this issue. As for Lebanon, we must get ready for a storm. Should the United States intervene, it would reinforce India's fear that our peaceful claims masked imperialist ambitions. It was time, the Ambassador concluded, to reevaluate our objectives and programs. The Russians and Chinese were active among the poorer classes. We could not afford to be complacent about the *status quo*.

Somehow the four days passed. Before the visitors went away, I learned that other hearts were as heavy as my own. One of the visiting officials decried the absence of any underlying principle, the unconcern about the assumptions on which budget decisions were based, the poverty of planning. But long experience with such meetings had made him phlegmatic. He had long ago given up hope that suggestions for betterment would be seriously considered.

Another senior officer urged me not to take the meeting to heart. It simply served as an excuse for the boys to get together, to indulge their egos and to cut up the pie. He pitied me for having to work under the Golf Links gun. He advised me to stay out of Headquarters' hair, and to pray that Headquarters would stay out of mine.

A veteran participant believed that the conference was just about what one had to expect. It was all a matter of tradition. Nowhere in the Agency, he felt, were creative men coming together in councils of war, sizing up problems, and pitting America's abilities and energies against her problems and opportunities abroad. Tradition ran, rather, in a contrary direction. The Agency's concerns were ingrown. Its outlook was parochial. Its methods were bureaucratic. Until a better example was set by the hierarchy, littler men had no choice but to go along, avoiding the controversy engendered by ideas, doing what they were told, and staying out of trouble. Here and there, a few persons with ideas and convictions thought, planned, wrote, communicated. Thanks to them, the show went on.

The weight that burdened my heart was not lifted by these answers. The fantastic performance remained unexplained. No one at the PAO meeting was a remittance man, exiled to stay out of sight and trouble. On the contrary, each had intelligence, presence, a way with people. Individually, they seemed representative of America. Collectively, their performance denied every quality in which America excelled.

No American educator worthy of the name would fail to examine the lessons of the past and consider their relevance to the present. Few American journalists would be so deficient in the talents of their craft as to produce publications of such patent crudity as ours. A businessman entering so precarious a field would surely research his market, pretest his plan, and perfect his product. No advertiser would fritter away his resources on such a charivari of ill-contrived and unconcerted output. No social scientist would be content to deal with local elites and American communication patterns, without ambition to learn about indigenous cultures and customs.

Baffled, I confided my puzzlement to Eadie. She came up with a clue. It was a little monthly magazine entitled *News Circle,* published by the American Women's Club in Delhi for its membership. The editors were wives of American officials in India: Bertie Meeker, Lois O'Neill, Margaret Stephenson, Martha Keehn, Chris Rosenfeld, Anne Bradley, Betty Sims, Barbara Maddux, Martha Cummings. Chitchat, book reviews, shopping tips, theater news, ads, a calendar of events, all happily illustrated by Jo Ann Boyd, seasoned more serious pieces about America and India. Unaffected, readable, enjoyable and useful, the little periodical harbored not a pica of propaganda in its twenty-four pages. Yet the image of America glowed in every line.

True, *News Circle* was edited for an American audience. But I got Eadie's point. *News Circle* had all the indispensable ingredients of successful communication missing in USIS output. It knew its audience. It satisfied the audience's interests. It was imbued with a sense of service. Not until USIS captured its humor, balance, brightness, and grace could the dormant talents of its staff come awake, conferring upon everything it did the benediction of American intelligence and integrity.

Despite the admissions of other officers and Eadie's understanding, I felt alone. How wise was it to have taken issue with Golf Links' position? In so ephemeral a field as public opinion, how could I know that I was right? Wearily, I walked the darkened streets of Delhi, gnawed by self-doubt. Unconsciously, my steps led toward Janpath. Under the arcade my friend the fortune teller huddled. I tiptoed past, but long fingers fastened themselves on my trouser-leg.

"Listen, sahib," he said. "Your name is known to me. It reveals the truth of your intention. But if you would be India's good friend, you must remember these magic words: 'The mind of the people is more powerful than the king as the rope made of many fibers is strong enough to drag a lion.'"

Parting with a rupee, I went home to bed.

IX. "For the welfare of all"

A Sister led me down the carbolic-scented corridor of
Holy Family Hospital. Helen Semmerling lay in an iron
bed beneath a crucifix, a forlorn figure with bright eyes,
a sweet smile, and a face yellowed by jaundice. Cecil
Auner, the Embassy doctor, had permitted me a brief
visit with the former Delhi PAO on my promise not to
talk shop. We chatted until the doctor arrived and ordered
me out. I waited for him in the lobby.

He said the prognosis had been grim, but Helen would
live. She had flown to Nepal in the pink of health. On the
return flight she contracted a cold. Other symptoms developed: ear blockage, fatigue, dysentery, loss of appetite.
Dr. Auner had taken one look and sent her to the hospital,
where she went into coma. A swift, accurate diagnosis and
prompt treatment had barely saved her life.

I asked the doctor how he had determined that hepatitis
was the basic disease, without being misled by all the
secondary symptoms. Cecil shrugged. "Experience, I sup-
pose. And after all, you know, medicine *is* a profession!"

Communication was also supposed to be a profession. I wished we had the same mastery of our field as the doctor had of his. If only we could see beyond the spots that blemished the American image; if only we could determine the essential flaw that twisted its features! The superficial symptoms could be treated in time. But to find the focus of infection, to cleanse away the fundamental fault—this was a test of true professionalism.

One by one, I considered the possibilities. Racism, for one. True, the Negro's failure to achieve first-class citizenship was a stain on the American image. But many Indians knew that the law was on the Negro's side, guaranteeing him an arena in which to wage his struggle. His strides from slavery were long and real. The very liveliness of the issue symptomized the vitality of freedom in America. Down deep, too, Indians knew that racism was not unique to America. The task of cleansing it was mankind's problem, and not solely America's.

Foreign policy, for another. True, America's role in world affairs was sometimes inept. But intelligent Indians understood that although every nation's foreign policy was directed toward its own self-interest, the United States was bringing to its foreign affairs new concepts of morality and generosity. America could not be all things to all men, backing every claim and cause. She could not salve sores that had festered since the Middle Ages.

The essential flaw was not militarism. True, a nation's supremacy in manpower, weaponry, and industrial war-making potential gave rise to fear among weaker nations. But never after World War II were America's conventional arms on a par with the Soviet Union's. As for our nuclear lead, it had proved all too transient. Russian rocketry, the streaking of Sputniks through outer space,

Khrushchev's bellicosity offset the image of a militant America.

Nor was it, on the other hand, American weakness. True, Sputniks sent America's stock tumbling while Russia's rose. But Indians who knew of the Soviet's lead in space were also aware of its failures in agriculture. America was being challenged, but its strength still commanded respect.

Neither was it materialism, nor cultural crudity, nor any weakness of character in the American people. No discerning Indian could see in his own people the indifference to worldly goods, the cultural grace, the purity of motive and action he found wanting in America.

These prejudices, certainly, distorted the American image in Asian minds. But all were variables that tended to cancel themselves out. Segregation riots debased America one day, but desegregation's ongoing drive went far to uplift it. American policy on Suez lessened Indian fears of our militarism, but a hint of American military action in Lebanon swiftly revived them. Sputniks made their mark, but the Salk vaccine revealed the exalted uses of science in which America excelled. Somehow, one had to search beyond the variables and find the constant that unbalanced the equation of Indian opinion.

That constant seemed to be capitalism.

Capitalism reminded quondam colonials of their centuries of slavery. In it they recognized the arch-foe of their efforts to be free. To many it was the motive force behind America's economic and military power: the force that threatened, except on Wall Street's terms, India's own development into a modern industrial state. Some envisaged it as the exploiter of their natural wealth, the profiteer enriching himself on the resale of their raw resources, the perpetuator of their impoverishment. To others, capitalism fueled the cheap but compelling culture that was inundating older civilizations, debasing values, and corrupting their youth.

Many intelligent Indians believed capitalism was a socially outmoded and morally indefensible element in American civilization. Having outlived whatever usefulness it might ever have had, it must now, they felt, give way to some more sensible social order. Even if they conceded capitalism's accomplishments in a country with rich resources, a literate population, and a dynamic culture, they doubted the system's applicability to poor, rural, illiterate societies seeking short cuts to industrialization and wealth.

Human dignity, freedom, the supremacy of the individual over the state—America's principles were impeccable. But to India they were irreconcilable with our capitalist economy. Failure to come to grips with this issue was interpreted as hypocrisy or evasion. As the gap in the American line—the sector we were least able to advance or defend—capitalism was the target for communism's heaviest fire.

Simply to mention capitalism was to close discussion. Indians winced at the word. Recognizing its loaded connotation, Americans were loath to use the term. Few Americans, moreover, could even define it. In Russell Davenport's words: "As America's curve of achievement has gone up, the curve of explainability has gone down."

Even those steady standbys, the USIS libraries, were of little help in tempering the antagonism toward American capitalism. Most books on the subject were either irrelevant to India or openly critical of the system. From *The Rise of Silas Lapham, The Octopus,* and *The Financier* to

The Grapes of Wrath, popular fiction dealt with the social consequences of capitalism with greater asperity than had Karl Marx. The waiting list for *The Organization Man, The Hidden Persuaders,* and *The Lonely Crowd* was long.

The ultimate danger implicit in any mention of capitalism derived, paradoxically, from its greatest virtue, the abundance it produced. In presenting to Indians evidence of American plenty, attention was focused on India's pitiless poverty. This tended to set up in the Indian mind a cause-and-effect relationship. India was poor *because* America was rich. The evidence of our affluence enforced the myth of capitalist exploitation. As David Potter put it in *People of Plenty:*

America's abundance has probably done more to cut us off from actual moral leadership than it has done to enhance such leadership, and certainly it has placed American generosity—much of which is both genuine and unselfish—under the curse of chronic envy.

Capitalism, in short, was central to the struggle between free and totalitarian systems. It could not be brushed beneath the rug. It had to be dealt with openly and honestly. The old injustices and inner contradictions described by Marx had to be replaced, in Indian minds, by a system compatible with the ideals the United States professed: a system, moreover, with positive meaning to India.

To identify capitalism as the fatal flaw in the American image abroad was one thing. To deal with it was another. One incident had sufficed to dramatize the American dilemma. Back home, the Advertising Council, an organization set up to place America's finest promotional talent at the public service, had also isolated anticapitalism as the focus of infection. With the blessing of the Administration, the National Association of Manufacturers, and the AFL-CIO, it had decided to deal with the problem head on, on the premise that pussyfooting would get nowhere. In association with the Information Agency, it had evolved a theme stressing the broad participation of the American people in producing, sharing, and enjoying the national wealth. Planning, hard work, saving, sacrifice, in an environment of freedom, were revealed as the factors underlying American abundance. The role of regulatory agencies, of social legislation, of investment, of competition, and of the consumer were underscored. The term applied to the project was "People's Capitalism." After exhibitions in Latin America and Ceylon had won kudos from the press, and recriminations from the Kremlin, "People's Capitalism" had been shipped to India.

The arrival of these exhibit materials had coincided with the arrival of an issue of *Foreign Affairs,* an American quarterly of political and economic commentary widely respected for the quality of its contributors. It contained an essay entitled "Rival Economic Theories in India." Criticizing the double standards Americans applied to their capitalist morals, the article took tooth and nail after "People's Capitalism." "All talk of People's Capitalism," the author wrote, "has little relevance to the United States, and no meaning at all for countries like India." Resting on "a bogus use of statistics," the entire thesis was labeled "synthetic—a pure distillate of boisterous enterprise and undiluted laissez-faire that comprised the common export version of American capitalism. To talk in India of the

virtue of capitalism, classical or modern, is to make little
or no contact with the realities of Indian economic life.
. . . It is becoming increasingly clear that Indian economic policy is at its best when it is most self-reliant."

The article had caused a minor sensation in the Indian
press. Its author was destined to become the next Ambassador of the United States to India, John Kenneth Galbraith.

For a year, the People's Capitalism exhibit had been
lying, boxed, in an empty lot outside USIS-India's Exhibits
Office. Costing thousands of dollars to conceive, to construct, and to ship, it was baked by the sun and drenched
by the rain. As though opening the crates might unleash
the very furies the exhibit was created to suppress, no one
went near the weathered pile. Passing this graveyard of
hard work and high hopes, I thought of an appropriate
epitaph, something Adolph Berle, Jr., had once written:
"Capitalism is not a philosophy for which to fight and die."

Like the mildewed crates, the issue wouldn't go away.
It demanded solution. One clue was supplied by the MIT
survey of "Indian Images of America" I had read upon
my arrival in Delhi. Henri Peyre, David Potter, and John
Galbraith provided others. Whatever form a solution took,
it seemed subject to four conditions:

First, it must not arouse Indian envy by parading our
prosperity before people unsure of their next day's bread.

Second, it must not solidify the stereotype in Indian
minds that life in America was dominated by materialism.

Third, it must not "sell" American capitalism to India;
rather, it must strive to harmonize the aspirations of India
and America in the economic field, relating American
experience to Indian conditions.

Fourth, it must avoid arguments induced by fanciful claims and by what Professor Galbraith termed "a bogus use of statistics." It must aim at one objective: to open Indian minds to a reconsideration of capitalism's case.

Analyzing the problem, my mind recalled an *ashram* in Segaon. I remembered Gandhi and the doctrine of *Sarvodaya:* "For the Welfare of All." At the time I had been struck by the parallel between Gandhi's economic idealism and American experimentation. Might *Sarvodaya* —For the Welfare of All—be the bridge on which India and America could meet?

Guided by Indian friends, I dug down to the wellsprings of Gandhi's inspiration, Vedanta. Between man and God, he reasoned, was unity. The gulf existing between the two was *avidya,* ignorance. The removal of this gulf was the goal of life: self-realization. Self-realization consisted of an understanding of self, of individual responsibility toward others, of advancing the good of all. Central to such advancement was the individual. Only the individual could bring about the inner change within himself which alone could regenerate society. The state could not make its citizens moral. Enforced morality was the denial of morality. Individual freedom and initiative were the bases of moral life.

This was the Vedic belief on which Gandhi built his economic thesis. Coupled with this belief was the conviction that the good of all could be achieved only by good means. Capital was good, not evil. Evil consisted in its wrong use. Capital in some form or other would always be needed. The wealthy man who supplied capital was worthy of respect. Society would be poorer if it lost the gifts of men who knew how to accumulate wealth. Also, the more widely economic power was dispersed, the better. Nothing could do society a greater disservice than to concentrate economic power in the State.

Gandhi believed in "the trusteeship of wealth." Wealth should be used for the good of each and all. Property was a condition necessary for the free play of individual ability. Those who possessed ability, however, should exercise it for the common benefit. The wealthy must not be dispossessed of their wealth. Rather, they should regard it as a trust, using it prudently for society's benefit. Where wealthy men failed in their responsibility as trustees, they must be educated and persuaded, not killed. Confiscation and violence could never be condoned. The *Sarvodaya* ideal could be achieved only by building up *Loka-Shakti*, the self-reliant power of the people dedicated to peaceful means of changing conditions.

Gandhi's ideals had a familiar ring. Faith in the individual. Belief in individual moral reform, in equality, in the dignity of labor. Industrialization to serve man, and not to exploit him. Division of the fruits of labor among those who produced them. Distrust of monopoly in any form—be it by government, by business, or by any majority or minority organization. Decentralization of power, self-help, voluntarism, and a parallel emphasis on social responsibility. Belief in a world of diversity, in which among the most precious freedoms was the right to disagree. Reliance on nonviolent means to reach ends centering on the welfare of all.

Not all Gandhi's ideals had become American actualities. But the gap between what the Mahatma preached and what America practiced was narrow enough to be bridged. Certainly no other society surpassed ours in its efforts to realize the classless society Gandhi envisaged. In this inner compatibility, perhaps, lay our hope.

Open to question, however, was the good taste of using Gandhi's name to advance understanding of American capitalism. To pre-test Indian reaction, I wrote an article for the Indian press. Essentially a personal testament, its purpose was to draw any adverse comment on the writer rather than on the American government. It recalled my first visit to India and my recognition of Gandhi's greatness. It quoted the Mahatma on the principles of *Sarvodaya*. Then, one by one, his ideals were related to the American scene:

A great sister democracy—the United States—stands shoulder to shoulder with India in its struggle toward prosperity, social justice and the self-fulfillment of its people. For the United States is dedicated, in heart, sinew, and soul, to many of the same ideals Gandhiji treasured. The United States too believes in and practices "the welfare of all." In American society the supreme consideration is man. To preserve human individuality—"the root of all progress"—is the cardinal tenet of the American way of life. Government, agriculture, industry—the entire society—is decentralized, with power spread as broadly as possible among the people. The people are masters of the state. The state is not the master of the people.

How America fulfilled Gandhi's ideas on the condition of labor, on economic equality, on a classless society was documented. As for Gandhi's doctrine of the Trusteeship of Wealth:

Taxes in America equalize wealth. Taxes are spent, as Gandhiji wished, to level up the living standards of the masses. Rich men give away part of their fortunes to serve mankind. The Rockefeller Foundation promotes the wellbeing of mankind throughout the world. The Ford Foundation furthers scientific, educational, and economic purposes for the public welfare. These are but two of thousands of similar organizations that give effect to Gandhiji's principle.

The article recognized that India was moving beyond many of Gandhi's fetishes. The contretemps between machinery and hand labor, between village self-sufficiency and modern industrialism, were frankly faced. Just as America was determined to maintain maximum freedom of economic action, so was India adjusting Gandhi's ideas to modern conditions.

The article concluded:

Indians call Gandhiji's principles Sarvodaya. Americans use different names. Politically, they call their way of life a democracy. Economically, they use words like "free enterprise," "a mixed economy," a "people's capitalism." But names do not matter so long as principles and goals remain the same. The means do not matter, so long as they are good—and so long as human individuality and freedom are preserved. True to their own traditions, Indians and Americans will pursue their own path, to their own destiny.

"God is Life, Truth, Love. He is the Supreme Good."

In this—Gandhiji's expression of his faith—America and India both believe. And it is in this belief that the two great sister democracies march toward Sarvodaya. Total uplift. The Welfare of All.

Major English, Hindi, and Urdu language dailies gave the piece prominence. Though it was distributed only in Delhi District, papers as far away as Calcutta's *Hind* and Jammu's *Ujjala* picked it up. The editorial reaction was favorable. The article also produced an avalanche of mail. A letter from Ambala typified the response:

I have read your articles: Sarvodaya, the Good of all. I am very delighted with the insight and understanding that you have shown in this excellent writing and am glad that now there is another American after Chester Bowles who has cared to study and understand the deep affinity between Indian outlook and tradition and American. My own pursuit of Indo-American kinship is based in the belief of the common ideals and outlook among the two people as brought out by you. I will suggest you to get this article reprinted in a pamphlet. We shall like to get some copies. Also we should start a symposium on the Indian-or-Gandhian-concept of Democracy. Let Democracy enkindle a new faith and purpose.

Universities, colleges, and secondary schools set up symposia on the economies of India and the United States. Organizations interested in international affairs invited us to address their memberships on modern trends in American capitalism. We entered Marxist thresholds hitherto closed, airing the outmoded nineteenth-century prejudices that underlay the anticapitalist case. Out of the experience, one lesson emerged: to open Indian minds to American viewpoints, we had first to open our minds to theirs.

The response encouraged us to make some broader use of the theme, recasting it in pictures and simple text for less literate audiences. We were considering the problems involved when a large young man with curly hair and a booming voice walked into the office. His name was Tom Hall Miller. Representing the Office of International Trade Fairs in Washington, his mission in New Delhi was to stage a display of American machinery suitable for small-scale industry. A gigantic dome was being built by the U.S. government on Mathura Road, the main thorough-fare linking the old and new cities of Delhi. Conceived by Tom to spur small-scale private enterprise requiring a minimum of capital, the exhibit lacked a theme. I told Tom about our experiment with *Sarvodaya*.

"For the Welfare of All" became the keynote of the small-scale industries exhibition. A series of photo-mural panels depicted the application of Gandhi's ideals in India and America. Tom employed a Hindi poet to compose a verse about machines at the service of man. At the en-trance to the exhibit, a troupe of classical Indian actors sang the words and danced to the strumming of *sitars*. *The New York Times* correspondent, reporting the in-augural night, termed this "singing commercial a high-light of the show that delighted hundreds of visitors." Noted too was "the series of panels behind whirring lathes and grinders quoting freely from Gandhi's teachings on the machine as a servant of mankind, on human freedom, on the dignity of honest labor, on the social responsibility of the rich and on social justice for the poor."

The Indian press also grasped and approved the mes-sage. "Is mechanization of production consistent with the Gandhian ideal of a decentralized economy?" asked *The Times of India*. "The U.S. Small Industries Exhibition an-swers in the affirmative. . . ." *The Statesman* missed none of the nuances implicit in the theme:

The exhibition highlights one of the main themes of Ameri-can life, that human hands and sweat can produce only a small fraction of the things that people need to live decently. Only machinery can satisfy the needs of the millions who inhabit the earth. In the background of the exhibits—products of eighty-two American manufacturers of tools, precision instruments, and machinery—are attractive placards and posters explaining how Mahatma Gandhi's ideals have been put into practice in America. Mahatma Gandhi believed, it is pointed out, that "machinery lightens the burden of the poor man," and that "it has come to stay." Also it stressed his belief that only in a free society can the poor prosper.

Over the ensuing months, several million Indians visited the Small Scale Industries Exhibition in Delhi, Bombay, Madras, and Calcutta. Some, presumably, came to know that American capitalism, like *Sarvodaya*, aimed at the welfare of all. In the process, other prejudices seemed to soften. One Indian spoke for many when he said: "*Sarvodaya* is proof of the understanding that serious study and genuine respect can bring about. Having come to a meeting of minds about capitalism, there is no problem Indians and Americans cannot resolve in a similar spirit."

Neither Delhi Post nor Tom Hall Miller had any illusions about the extent of our success. "For the Welfare of All" was barely the beginning of something that needed to be said, again and again, at every level of Indian society. Other minds, doubtless, would find ways to say it better. All we had done was to isolate the anticapitalist germ and to satisfy the four conditions for dealing with it.

We had not aroused Indians' envy by flaunting our abundance in their faces.

We had not reinforced the Indian conviction that life in America is materialistic.

We had harmonized India's and America's economic outlook.

Avoiding argument over "bogus statistics," we had opened a few Indian minds to a reconsideration of the case for capitalism.

Having met the test, "For the Welfare of All" was ready for wider exposure to the India lying beyond the four largest cities to which Tom Miller had taken it. Redesigned as a series of panels fitted into a Chevrolet truck, with a wealth of descriptive pictures relating American experience to the realities of Indian life, it was proposed as a touring exhibit.

But Golf Links distrusted the undertaking, labeling it "un-American" and—rather oddly, I thought—"propaganda." The "People's Capitalism" crates were opened. Their contents were also adjudged "unusable, physically and psychologically, for use in India." An exhibit was then created to satisfy the requirements of the situation as USIS-India saw it.

Christened "Life in America: a Progressive Economy," it stressed materialism as the essence of American civilization.

Bolstered with statistics on which American economists themselves disagreed, its claims aroused argument.

Shunning any reference to the problems peculiar to India, it dealt exclusively with the superiority of the American system.

Crowned with a gleaming refrigerator and other push-button appliances, it advertised American abundance.

Packed into a caravan of trucks, the exhibit set forth to sell "Life in America" to people who eked out their existence on incomes averaging a dollar a week.

x. Monsoon

Cumulus clouds swept up from the Indian Ocean, darkening Delhi's skies. The air thickened with moisture and the perfume of flowering shrubs. Occasionally black winds blew in from the west, rattling windows, toppling trees, and dumping tons of dust from the Rajasthan desert. Or an awesome stillness seized the city, with not a leaf stirring and even the hoopoes hushed. Eyes gazed with hope and dread at sunsets like cathedral windows, multicolored, with shafts of sunshine piercing the gloom. Then the monsoon broke. Giant buckets of water doused Delhi, flooding the streets, stalling traffic, turning the open sewers into rampaging rivers.

With the monsoon came the climax in Lebanon. At 4 P.M., Tuesday, July 15, 1958, a telephone call summoned me to Golf Links. To a small group gathered in his office, the Country PAO confided that United States Marines were expected to land on the beaches off Beirut that night. At the worst, the action invited world war. At the least, it dealt a body blow to Indo-American relationships, undoing all efforts over the years to convince India of America's devotion to peace. By midnight the news would be out. We had only a few hours to make our plans to meet the Indian reaction.

The group included most of Golf Links' ranking officers. The only new face was that of the former Bombay PAO, recently arrived to replace the Deputy who had been promoted to the top USIS spot in a neighboring country. Confidence in the solidity of Indo-American ties, so optimistically asserted in the PAO conference a few weeks before, had vanished. It was replaced by the certainty of Indian wrath. The group agreed that all USIS could do in the circumstances was to step up the flow of news releases to the Indian press, giving the American side of the story as relayed by wireless from Washington. The *American Reporter* would play a major role, publishing official texts on the American position. As for such activities as film showings, exhibits, and cultural events, these had best be canceled to avoid incidents. Meanwhile, measures must be taken to protect American life and property. The Country PAO said that security officers from the Embassy would inspect our premises and inform us of what must be done in case of demonstrations. It was agreed that secrecy be maintained until midnight, after which we could break the news to our families and staff.

Golf Links had not underestimated India's anger. It was prompt, passionate, and unanimously anti-American. Mobs marched on the American Embassy. Cordons of police held them outside the gates. Upraised fists and placards vowed death to Yankee imperialists. Communists sparked the tumult in the streets, but they could not be credited with the anti-American spasm that shook the press. The very journalists most sedulously pursued by USIS were among the most irate.

"Another Suez!" trumpeted the *Indian Express* in an editorial paralleling our action in Lebanon with the French-British-Israeli attack on Egypt. Other articles equated Beirut with Budapest, seeing no difference in the brutality of American and Soviet interference in another nation's internal affairs. "No wonder India reacts so strongly to American action in Lebanon," wrote a typical fair-weather friend. "Maybe that is because we too have a feeling of having been wronged by the U.S.A. We in this country cannot forget the U.S. stand on Kashmir. They justify their intervention in the civil war in Lebanon, but fail to appreciate our defense of Kashmir—which lawfully acceded to us and became part of our country—against open, admitted foreign aggression."

It was a chastening experience to be in a foreign country during an anti-American siege. To say good-by to one's family in the morning, unsure of what the day might bring; to watch while secret files were removed by Marine guards to a place of safety; to listen as security officers pointed out escape routes down fire escapes, over rooftops, via distant alleys; to visit the USIS library, wondering whether to risk pillage by remaining open, or, by closing the doors, to advertise an American defeat—all these had been unimaginable prior to the event. Now we breathed antipathy in the air.

On Virgil Groom fell the major burden. For forty-eight hours he never closed his eyes. His press section worked in eighteen-hour shifts. As the news cascaded from the teletype, Vic Kulanday's staff translated it into Hindi, Rajasthani, Punjabi, and Urdu. Typists tapped out the edited texts. In the basement, mimeograph machines clattered night and day. The office jeep, dubbed the "Red Ball Express," careened through the streets, delivering reams of USIS releases to local editors. Sacks of mail were deposited at the Post Office for out-of-Delhi distribution.

The heart-breaking effort was futile. Editors preferred commercial news sources to the propaganda agency of an involved alien power. The Press Trust of India, Reuters, the Agence France Presse—none friendly to the American position—captured the headlines. While President Eisenhower's statement to Congress got a good play, as did Ambassador Lodge's address to the United Nations, USIS output hardly saw the light of print. A paragraph in a widely read column in an English language daily twitted us for our efforts. It told of an Indian editor collapsing into bed early one morning after a long night's labors. Awakened by a frantic knocking at the door, he dashed downstairs in the darkness at the risk of his neck. Outside, the Red Ball Express was disappearing down an alley. On the doorstep was a packet labelled URGENT! Opening it, he found yet another USIS handout, its news one day late.

My first reaction was that editorial intransigence doomed any hope of presenting America's case. But a comparison of articles featured in the Indian press, set alongside USIS output, tended toward a contrary conclusion. The blame for the embargo might lie less with Indian editors than with USIS. Editors saw Lebanon against the panorama of history. We dished out daily news, often a day or more late. They reacted to Lebanon with the revolutionary reflexes of a people but recently freed from colonialism. We gave the impression of defending the *status quo*. They wanted the careful style of a gifted writer, the profundity of a thinker, the insights of a scholar. We ground out journalese—a short lead paragraph followed by terse explanatory text. They wanted service they couldn't get from commercial sources—statements from high American sources dealing with events in a manner considerate of Indian opinion. We thought of "service" in terms of a Red Ball Express.

I tried my hand at a piece patterned to Indian specifications. It strove to be a statesmanlike exposition of the American case, written from the heart rather than from a handout originating half a world away. I visualized its author as the most eminent American in Asia—the United States Ambassador to India. Closest to Asian audiences, he was the American official most able to harmonize the American action with Asian self-interest, to explain it in terms Asians could comprehend.

Should the Indian press refuse to publish the text, one other means of reaching Asian audiences remained. The Ambassador could commit his words to tape. Flown to Washington, they could be translated into every Asian tongue. Broadcast by the Voice of America, the statement could hurdle the prejudices of a hostile press, reaching audiences all over Asia without censorship or distortion.

The statement set out to do four things. The first was to make clear America's appreciation of Indian sensitivities:

. . . Here in India, the impact of America's action has been strong. To anyone who knows India, this response is natural. It stems directly from the centuries-old philosophy of nonviolence, of peace, of justice, of brotherly love so eloquently affirmed in the modern world by Gandhiji. . . . The ideals cherished and preserved throughout India's long history are shared by the people of the United States. We, too, understand the meaning of Janata Janardana— "the People are God." We, too, believe that Dharma or law is sovereign. We, too, are disciples of the Vedic ideal, abhorring tyranny, injustice and bloodshed. We, too, know the humiliation, the suffering, the ardor of the urge to independence which colonialism inspires. We, like you, in Shri Nehru's words are "children of revolution," conditioned by the same inheritance—a revolutionary spirit which still governs our activities.

The second purpose of the statement was to place the Lebanese action in the perspective of time, and to establish its consistency with the American character. From 1776 to 1958, the American record was traced in the Western hemisphere, China, the Philippines, Europe, Africa, and India. Unwaveringly, the United States had supported the self-determination of peoples of every race, creed, and color. In the same tradition that caused America to support India's independence movement, we had midwifed the birth of twenty other nations since the end of World War II. In Iran, Greece, and Korea the United States had resolutely defended the territorial integrity and independence of small nations, even as, today, it defended the liberties of Lebanon.

The third purpose of the statement was to reveal the American record vis-à-vis Arab nationalism:

History reveals that for four hundred years the Arab peoples were subject to foreign domination, and almost sealed off from the outside world. Not until the nineteenth century, under the rule of Ibrahim Pasha, were French and American missionaries permitted in the Lebanon. Then, from the ideals of the French and American revolutions, came the inspiration for an intellectual and political renaissance that swept the Mediterranean from Alexandria to Aleppo. Its propagator was a college, founded in 1866, and destined to become famous throughout the world as the American University of Beirut. It is said that more than 75 per cent of all Arab leaders today are products of the American University. Here, in short, in an American university, Arab nationalism found a father and a friend.

How Woodrow Wilson espoused the Arab cause; how American pressure helped free Syria, Lebanon, and Egypt; how America's prompt intercession in November, 1956, preserved Egypt's territorial integrity—these were recalled as examples of dedication to principle, elevated above blind loyalty to friends.

The final purpose of the proposed Ambassadorial statement was to restate the American position in Lebanon in an Indian perspective. India's sponsorship in the United Nations of the "Peace through Deeds" resolution was recalled. It was upon this very resolution that America's action was predicated.

The statement was long, but I resisted the urge to cut. Its length, indeed, was part of the test. Hundreds of short USIS releases had wound up in waste baskets. On the other hand, my lengthy article on *Sarvodaya* had gleaned a heavy harvest. Once again I was inclined to rely on India's sense of fair play.

I called the Country PAO and said I had an urgent matter to discuss. He invited me over right away. He listened to the plan and read the statement. A glacial man, he seemed to thaw. Picking up his Deputy, we headed for the Embassy.

In the office of the Political Counsellor, I presented my plan to break the Indian press embargo. The Deputy shook his head. No editor would print anything so long. To send out so bizarre a statement was not in the USIS tradition.

The Political Counsellor said the most precious asset we had was the Ambassador's personal standing with the Prime Minister. To jeopardize it by such a statement might be a mistake. Lebanon would blow over in time. Meanwhile the less we did to fan the flames, the better.

The decision rested with the Country PAO. He said he agreed with their views. He couldn't see the Ambassador, widely known for his sincerity but not learned in the Indian classics, making such a speech. He thought "USIS would be on firmer ground if it stuck to facts, instead of appealing to Indian emotions."

The next day the Ambassador called a meeting to discuss the emergency. He led off by describing the reaction of the Prime Minister and other Indian officials to the American landings. Though individually they were outraged by the intervention, the Indian government was pursuing a moderate line. Pressures from the Communist bloc, urging Nehru to denounce American imperialism, were being resisted. But Lebanon was a terrible test of the true quality of Indo-American amity. It revealed that despite American aid and other evidence of our friendship, Indians were quick to suspect our intentions.

After reviewing the latest communiqués from Washington and Beirut, where a question mark still hovered over the beaches, the Ambassador asked for our comments. The consensus was to lie low, to let events take their natural course, and to wait for the dust to settle.

I entered a dissent. I said this was one of those occasions when valor might be the better part of discretion, and when men of conviction should not submit in silence to the calumny heaped on the United States. Aside from the President himself, only one man could speak for America in India. The Ambassador was that man. Four days had passed since the landings. India's accusations had all been aired. Except for a nationwide broadcast of President Eisenhower's statement on the American position, arranged by Golf Links' resourceful radio officer, America's answers were ignored by India's radio and press. This was the time for the Ambassador to lay his prestige on the line. If he would plead America's case, all Asia would listen. If he didn't, the dust indeed would settle. But the precious moment would pass when the right word by the right man might moderate Indian opinion, or even swing it to our side, carrying with it much of Asia's.

The only sound in the room was the splash of rain on the windows. My words, I knew, had come close to lese majesty. It was a moment when, I hoped, the Country PAO would submit the text itself, inviting a careful reading on which a judgment might be based. Instead, the Deputy repeated his opinion that the idea was worthless. The Country PAO agreed. Without USIS support, the proposal foundered. The decision was to prepare a summary of President Eisenhower's address to Congress for the Ambassador's signature, for publication in the *American Reporter*.

Back at my office, I wrote the Country PAO a note. I said that long before Lebanon, Delhi Post had scheduled an exhibition in Kanpur, a large industrial city in Uttar Pradesh. Audiences expected an American speaker. Despite the current ban on public appearances, I felt that I should keep the appointment. I also asked whether he had any objections to my releasing the Lebanon statement to the Indian press, over my own signature.

The Country PAO replied that he had no objections to keeping the Kanpur schedule if I was willing to accept the risks. As for the statement on Lebanon: "I doubt that any

editor would print it in its entirety, if at all. I would not try
to publish such a piece at this time and in this way."

I studied the reply. It did not seem to prohibit my sending out the statement on my own. I handed it to Virgil and
asked him to release it to the local press.

The only other passenger in my compartment was a thin
blond man from the Polish Embassy. I offered him a
Camel. He scowled and turned his back. I gazed out the
window at a liquid landscape. As far as my eye could pene-
trate the murk, India was a mass of mud. Across the horizon, palm trees stood upended like frazzled mops. Water
stood high in village streets, dissolving buildings and turning the fluted dung cakes into slime. Stations flashed by
with ads for Passing Show cigarettes, featuring a monocled
man in a topper. In the refuge of scabrous temples from
the Gupta era, monkeys copulated or glumly watched the
rain.

The Pole, as though contaminated by my presence, left
the compartment. I stretched out on the seat, wondering
whether nonviolence was more than a word in the Hindi
language. Kanpur was a textile town in deep depression;
communism was rife among the unemployed. To them
Lebanon was one more example of capitalist aggression
that kept mankind in misery.

The train whistle blew incessantly, its mournful hoot
mingling with the monsoon's howl. We were passing
through a forest. The lush trees were gnarled, twisted, can-
cerous, with amputated limbs and big black holes like
toothless mouths or eyeless sockets. And then, once more,
the endless fields.

Yash Gupta from my office was waiting for me at Kanpur

station. His handshake was warm, but his spirits were troubled. He had searched for a location for our exhibition in the center of the city, but a Polish presentation of folk art had been given preference. He had finally set up our display in a schoolroom in the outskirts of the town. Even with the addition of potted plants and colored streamers, he said the effect was dismal. The Polish show beat ours hands down. Nevertheless, audiences were looking forward to a chance to meet an American. Record turnouts at all my talks were expected. The first was a tea with members of the local press at the Berkeley Hotel where a room had been reserved. Yash said it was run by the only pro-American in Uttar Pradesh, a Zoroastrian, who could be entrusted with my safety.

About twenty correspondents awaited me at the Berkeley. For almost an hour we stood around the table, sipping tea and exchanging polite conversation. The atmosphere was reserved. A tray of *pan* was passed around. *Pan* is the Indian equivalent of spearmint gum and chewing tobacco —a leaf smeared with lime, betel, and assorted spices, and garnished, on ceremonial occasions such as this, with silver foil. I loathed *pan,* not only for its taste, but because it induced a flow of crimson-stained saliva. Fearing that a refusal might seem unfriendly, I placed a wad inside my cheek.

The dean of the local corps led off the inquisition. A big man with a bald head, thick eyeglasses, and a *dhoti* whose crispness defied the weather, he said he was more concerned with India than with Lebanon. "Despite Pandit Nehru's repeated warnings that American military aid encourages Pakistan against India and is an unfriendly act against us, America gives aid to our enemy. Dictator Ayub

Khan has openly threatened India with war. How can America be friendly to India when she is arming Pakistan?"

I rose to reply, but my mouth was filled with spittle. I looked for a receptacle in which to eject the bitter stuff, but none was at hand. For several seconds I struggled for a way to ease my embarrassment, fearing nausea if I swallowed the *pan*, and unable to reply if I did not. The silence was interpreted as inability to answer the question. Other newsmen moved in for the kill.

"Russia has openly declared Kashmir as a part of India. Why does not America do so?"

"Mr. Dulles has stated that Goa is a province of Portugal. How do you explain this?"

"India stands for *Panch Sheel*, peaceful coexistence. The United States stands for military pacts. How can our friendship develop in this contradictory situation?"

The questions climaxed on the central issue: the world's desire for disarmament, coexistence, peace—opposed by American "brinkmanship," of which Lebanon was the latest example.

Gulping down the *pan*, I pointed out that the United States maintained its armed forces for one purpose: to avoid war by deterring aggression. We had no designs on the territory or wealth of others. We armed only in order to convince potential aggressors that resort to force or subversion would be an unprofitable adventure. We used armed force only, as in Lebanon, to preserve the sovereignty of nations incapable of protecting themselves. Wherever there were American forces overseas, it was in response to pleas of the host nation for our help.

The dean of correspondents bluntly stated that he didn't believe me. "You are paid to say these things! And you say so much, your words have no meaning!" His colleagues clapped.

Seven other talks were scheduled. Everywhere, the same correspondents, led by their dean, showed up. Questions never varied from the press tea pattern. Audiences didn't deeply care about Lebanon. Lebanon was simply a handy peg on which to hang India's gripes on Goa, Kashmir, arms aid to Pakistan. My answers made no impression. Indeed, based on American premises, and unrelated to Indian interests, they were worse than no answers at all.

Midway in the schedule I changed my tactic. In 1954, I said, the United States had offered arms aid programs to India and Pakistan. As was its right, India refused. As was its right, Pakistan accepted. In supplying such aid to Pakistan, the President of the United States made it clear that if ever Pakistan attacked India, the United States would be on India's side. That promise still held. It was a matter of record. It would be kept.

But arms aid to Pakistan, I said, wasn't the central issue. The central issue was collective security. India objected to America's alliance with Pakistan, its pacts with Portugal and other nations. It doubted our objective: to preserve world peace through collective security. Collective security was not an American idea. The first example in human history of peoples joining together in common defense against aggression was Indian. The Battle of the Ten Kings described in the Rig Veda revealed that so long as Indian tribesmen fought separately, India was easy prey. Only when men and arms were grouped in units, presenting a united front to the foe, was India strong and free.

I recalled how India's ancient sage, Shukracharya, had described the Indian strategy on the eve of the Turkish and Afghan invasions. Villages combined in *samitis* for mutual defense against foreign invaders. *Yamiks* stood guard, armed and paid from a common fund. Each village owned a certain number of weapons, and these, with officers and men, were joined in pacts to resist invasion. Later, in the thirteenth century, records once again revealed that relationships between village republics were based on mutual aid rather than mutual exclusiveness. As long as India's villages maintained collective security arrangements, India threw back aggressors. When the villages were divided, India fell.

The dean of correspondents looked angry, but I went on. Benjamin Franklin, I said, was the first American to borrow the Indian idea. Facing revolution against Great Britain, he warned that "we must all hang together or most assuredly we will all hang separately." By hanging together—by collective security—the colonies won their struggle, and America became free. Decades of neutralism and isolationism followed. They taught us, at bitter cost, that by ourselves we could not deter aggression. Only now, after World War II and Korea, were we joining with others in *samitis* of mutual defense.

The audience's applause was perfunctory. The sole comfort was that Indians were nonviolent and willing to listen. A few shook my hand, and as if to ease the tension, asked questions about education, Marilyn Monroe, and other features of the American scene. One, the presiding officer at a meeting of Kanpur's Foreign Policy Association, was effusively friendly. Introducing me to the packed room in an interminable speech, he referred to my business acumen, which had made me a wealthy man, to the excellence of the textiles I manufactured, which rivaled Kanpur's, and to my intimate connections with the leading figures of the Republican administration. Then he turned to me, held out his hand, and said: "It is a pleasure to welcome to Kanpur the well-known Bernard Goldfine!"

The inaugural night of the United States exhibition in Kanpur coincided with the height of the monsoon. Wind and rain buffeted the city. Water six inches deep surrounded the out-of-the-way schoolhouse in which the display was housed. A few naked light bulbs accentuated the gloom.

It was my first experience with a USIS exhibit. The theme was hard to discern. It turned out to be a series of photographs taken by Asian students in the United States. The pictures were small, about eight inches by ten, and lengthy captions were printed in illegible type. Hanging individually from the walls, they fluttered and drooped in the gale.

Though it was well past the hour appointed by the invitations, the room was empty. I half hoped no one would come. The exhibit ill repaid anyone brave enough to leave a dry house that stormy night. I grieved that America, so versed in the graphic arts, should mount such a monstrous show. I grieved, too, at my own folly in coming to Kanpur. For all my pretensions, I had made no friends.

I was about to suggest to Yash that we close the doors and go back to the Berkeley when the sound of a bicycle was audible outside. I heard someone anchor it to a lamp post. Footsteps sloshed through the water and up the steps. Into the room walked a big man with a bald head and thick-lensed glasses, wielding a wet umbrella like a club. His *dhoti* was sodden and plastered with mud. It was the dean of the local corps of correspondents. I braced for another outburst, but the man's face broke into a smile, half rueful, half friendly.

"I cycled across the city," he said, "to tell you that I think you are sincere. I believe what you said about your country."

Tom Allen, Jack Maddux, and Virgil Groom greeted me in Delhi with news that the press blackout had been broken. Our statement on Lebanon had been published in leading English, Hindi, Punjabi, and Urdu papers. Even the *Indian Express,* which had termed American intervention "Another Suez!" had labeled it "a lucid presentation of the American view both on relations with India and on recent events in West Asia." Weeklies, including such respected publications as *The Eastern Economist, Current,* and *Thought,* had devoted entire pages to it.

One publication had turned it down: the *American Reporter.* Appearing the day after the landings in Lebanon, the *Reporter* had featured stories about Alaskan Statehood, the Vacuum Tube of Lee De Forest, American Aid to Indian Highways, and a full-page illustrated article entitled "Dioramas Create Scenes from American History." Then a special Lebanon edition had been rushed to press. Appearing July 23, it carried the speeches of the President and Ambassador Lodge, both of which Indian newspapers had played up eight days earlier. A box on page one contained a summary of these speeches under the Ambassador's name.

The Ambassador's prestige had, after all, been committed. The Embassy of the United Arab Republic, it seemed, had accused the United States of forging evidence of subversion in Lebanon to justify its intervention. Good public relations policy suggested that the absurd charges be ignored. But USIS had dignified them with a release containing the American Ambassador's denial.

Golf Links, in addition, had produced the first issue of a new publication in India. Entitled the *American Embassy Newsletter*, it was a four-page affair written in the staccato style of the Kiplinger letter, underscoring key sentences and giving in capsule form the American position on domestic and foreign affairs. In addition to the *American Reporter*, it would henceforth be mailed regularly to India's elite.

XI. The common man

Amid fields of sugar cane, mustard, and barley, the village of Sagar slept in the sun. Under the mango trees, big-domed and short-stemmed like giant green toadstools, huddled the house of the headman, the mud-walled homes of the clean castes, the hovels of the untouchables. In the dusty lanes coppersmiths, bustards, and scrawny chickens pecked at refuse flung from the village's seventy-seven kitchens. Atop a house-high cone of dung cakes, disc-shaped, fluted and finger-marked with loving artistry, a peacock preened, warbling "no-no-no" in a passionate contralto. Near the whitewashed temple, a girl tugged the udders of a bony cow. Beyond, a cluster of women chattered while waiting to fill great brass urns with sweet water from the well.

Sagar was one of the 154 villages in the Development Block of Girwa, carved out of the district surrounding the lake-city of Udaipur in Rajasthan. Its people were Bhils, aboriginal farmers, their holdings averaging about four acres per family. Though each of India's half-million vil-

lages was in some respect distinctive, Sagar had characteristics common to almost all. Eight citizens out of ten were
illiterate and in debt, paying the local moneylenders up to
40 per cent annually in interest. Nowhere in the village
was there a bathroom or latrine. The smell of excrement
hung in the air. Malaria, guinea worm, and pneumonia
bit deeply into the population of 782 persons. Yet despite
the absence of medical care—the nearest dispensary was
at Barapal, eleven miles away, and presided over by an
untrained clerk—births overtook deaths by about forty
mouths a year.

To a visitor's eye, the hamlet seemed as stagnant as the
half-dry *sagar* or waterhole which gave the place its
name. But in reality the village pulsed with life. From a
schoolroom came the voices of children singing:

A new national regime has been established.
The kingdom has been captured by the white-capped Gandhiji.
In Delhi Shri Nehru is working for the people.
The king of Mewar called the people to defend his kingdom.
The people refused to help the king.
The people favor freedom.

In the bazaar, a battery-powered radio divided the day
into music, tips to farmers, drama, and news. Decalcoma-
nias advertised Dalda ghee, India's mass-produced cook-
ing grease, and Hindustan Lever's Lux. Six bicycles, one
Gramophone, a sewing machine, a petrol pump dispensing kerosene—these also reflected changes wrought by industrialization in Sagar's way of life. So did its three status
symbols: ball point pens, sunglasses, and machine-made
cigarettes.

A road linked the village with Udaipur, the capital, sixty

miles south. Every evening a bus stopped outside the tea stall, dropping off newspapers, an occasional piece of mail for the headman, and sometimes a passenger. A government official, perhaps, to discuss taxes with the local land recorder. Or the Village Level Worker, eager to interest the farmers in some new idea. Evidence of his earlier visits was everywhere—in improved seeds, green manure, pest controls, chemical fertilizers that, used with the *kharif* crops sown in the last rainy season, had sent the harvest of cowpea, cotton, and corn soaring.

Sometimes it was a holy man who seized the citizens' imaginations for a fortnight with a religious preachment, turning their superstition to his own advantage until sanity was restored. Sometimes it was a cinema—a Government of India documentary screened by an Information Officer, or an entertainment film made in Bombay, Moscow, Peking, or Hollywood. For weeks afterward, villagers compared the customs of the outside world as revealed by these celluloid self-images. Sometimes it was a traveling troupe of players who, along with song and dance, amused audiences with topical fare. "Take comfort, brothers," a clown would cry. "America is sending us help. The shot fired across the frontier from Pakistan—that is American aid to India!"

This day it was a simple peasant who held Sagar in the grip of his tongue. His name was Ram Dhar, an unassuming little man who farmed a *biswa* of rented land on the road to Eklinggi. Two days earlier he had left for Udaipur, laden with guavas to sell in the city. Now he dropped off the bus, his produce sold, a new silver ear cleaner and toothpick dangling from his neck. In one hand, a kerchief bulged with packages purchased for friends. The other fist clutched a sheaf of newspapers. The men in the tea stall, squatting on benches and picking at their toenails, moved over to give him room. "Hanh," said the land recorder, "how did it go? What is news in the city?"

Beads of sweat broke out on the farmer's brow, less from the heat than from embarrassment. To command every eye and ear was an unaccustomed honor.

"Panditji"—Prime Minister Nehru—"sent an ambassador to America," he said. "Now he has come home. There is a big *tamasha* in Udaipur celebrating his arrival. Many pictures and words tell what he saw in that country. In the evening there was a cinema. There actually was a man in Udaipur who claimed to be an American!"

"Who was this man?" the grain merchant asked.

"Oh, a well-fed fellow like a Maharajah's son, and pale like an Englishman. But pleasant enough, full of laughter, without great airs. I understood nothing he said, but others explained that according to him, common men like ourselves rule America."

"That is a lie," growled the pan dealer. "Everyone knows that America is ruled by usurers, soldiers, and bandits."

Ram Dhar shrugged. "Perhaps. But Panditji's ambassador who was sent to spy out the land said that these reports about America are not true. For all their different ways, they are much the same as we. True, in America, houses are made of wood, not mud. The people work in fields divided by iron wire, and not cactus as here. They too have Moghul towers made of stone, but they fill their towers with machines and women to run them. Sweat is no stranger there. For the rest"—Ram Dhar spread several newspapers on the table—"it is all here. Perhaps the schoolmaster will read it so all can listen."

Caught in the spotlight of Sagar's curiosity, the teacher

polished his spectacles, dragging out the operation until the barber whipped out his razor. "Will anyone have a shave?" he cried. "Your beards grow long while you wait." The teacher's voice, stumbling over the Hindi script, subdued the laughter.

"It says that Panditji's ambassador was awed by the vastness and wealth of America. But mostly he noticed the friendliness of the people. The common men and women of America are simple, God-fearing, and unselfish. The secret of their wealth is that they are not always looking over their shoulders to the past. Their eyes are on the future. They are practical. They believe in doing things, in improving their lives, in putting the soil, forest, and seas to their service. Above all, they work hard. Even the rich do not expect rough work to be done by servants. No one looks down on work as being beneath his caste."

As the teacher read, he pointed to pictures in the newspapers. The group hovered over his finger, eying every detail of the houses, the clothes, the work habits of ordinary Americans. The teacher's eyes lit up as he recognized a familiar face. "That is Abraham Lincoln," he announced. "He is the Gandhi of America. He freed the slaves. Government of the people, by the people, for the people—those were his words!"

Cynicism drew down the corners of the headman's lips. "Only socialism is government by and for the people. In America they have capitalism. Capitalism does not free people. It enslaves them."

The teacher's head wobbled in dissent. "Panditji's ambassador reports that American capitalism has changed. People own their land and shops. Railroads, mills, dams, other great enterprises are either owned by the common people, or they are built or controlled for their benefit by the government. Listen to the ambassador's words: 'Whatever one's views on capitalism, it remains true that in America wealth and *dharma* go together. The rich must use their wealth for the general welfare. The results can be seen all over the land—in schools, hospitals, roads, and places where people play. Women share these things equally with men.' "

The teacher paused to decipher the caption beneath the final picture. "Like common men everywhere Americans want peace."

"The Common Man in America" was Delhi Post's first effort to communicate with the common man in India. It was based on a speech delivered on All-India radio by G. L. Mehta, for more than five years India's ambassador to the United States. What Americans could not say about themselves without violating Indian values of modesty and humility, the perceptive ambassador had said eloquently, honestly, convincingly to his own people.

I had met Ambassador Mehta years before in Manchester, New Hampshire, in the course of a trip he had made through the New England states. The local Council on World Affairs, of which I was a director, had invited him to participate in a TV broadcast. I had joined him and other panelists in a lively discussion of Indian life. American attitudes toward caste, asceticism, neutralism, and the like were put forth by the participants. Mr. Mehta replied with a remarkable grasp of just the right allusion, drawn from American experience, to make India meaningful to a Yankee audience. For weeks after, my telephone rang with messages from friends—garage mechanics, farmers, housewives, high school students—asking me to relay their thanks to the Indian Embassy. A nurse in the Concord

Hospital voiced a general sentiment: "Thank God that the means are being made available for people to get to know each other, and that nations are trying to reach each other with information and ideas instead of guns. Listening to a flesh-and-blood Indian has changed my entire outlook on his country."

Now it fell my way to follow in Mr. Mehta's footsteps, bringing some knowledge of America to the ordinary people of India. "Panditji's Ambassador" readily consented to the use of his speech for such a purpose. Utilizing photographs in the office morgue, supplied by a young Nisei genius named Yoichi Okamoto who headed the Agency's photo unit, the Ambassador's key phrases were illustrated with photographs, and the entire speech converted into a mobile exhibit. Light enough to fit into the Chevrolet truck owned by Delhi Post, the unit's merits lay largely in its uncluttered design, the clarity of its photographs, and the simplicity of its English and Hindi captions.

The exhibit was but one element in an integrated approach to the problem of communicating with India's masses. A second element was an American speaker. Picking up each point made by Mr. Mehta, Jack Maddux fleshed it out in a series of talks. One described the political and social aspects of modern American capitalism. Another dwelt on labor, with emphasis on collective bargaining and other instruments evolved by government, management, and labor. A third talk dealt with the right of all men to participate in their country's cultural life, rather than the limitation of its benefits to a small aristocracy. It enumerated the strengths and weaknesses of a middle-class culture. A fourth described the role of women in American life, from colonial times to the present, substituting reality for the frivolous floozy conjured up by cer-

tain books, magazines and films. Other talks strove to balance the negative stereotypes highlighted by surveys of
Indian opinion. All stressed the spiritual basis for hard
work, sacrifice, producing and sharing in American civilization. De-emphasized were the differences in the material status of the two peoples. Like Ambassador Mehta's
in Manchester, our message dealt with the compatibility
of Judeo-Christian, Hindu, and Islamic beliefs, and the
wide areas of experience and aspiration we held in common. Together with an illustrated pamphlet incorporating
Ambassador Mehta's original address, all texts were translated into Hindi, Urdu, and Punjabi idioms.

How to reach India's common man with our message
remained the crux of our problem. To visit the thousands
of villages where he dwelt was out of the question. Our
only hope lay in the larger communities around which
rural life revolved. Night after night, lights blazed in Tom
Allen's office as he, Gus Gujral, and Basil Monier hovered
over maps, searching for the special combination of factors essential for our purpose. Those factors included, first,
a university, college, or system of schools, including agricultural institutions and training centers for Village Level
Workers. Second, indigenous organizations, such as Indo-
American cultural societies, labor unions, Rotary clubs,
farmers', youths', and women's groups able to provide a
forum for the widest dissemination of our message. Third,
sites of country fairs, market places, trading centers, religious and other celebrations patronized by the peasantry.
Fourth, offices of vernacular newspapers and magazines
with circulations in rural areas. Fifth, a sponsoring group,
respected by all elements of local society. Forty-nine communities qualified. Among them was Udaipur.

Three weeks before "The Common Man" was slated to

open in that city, Gus Gujral swung aboard the Udaipur Express. His task was to set the stage for an Indo-American cultural week centered around the exhibit, film shows, and an American speaker. His first problem was to gain the District Commissioner's consent. Pleased by the choice of Udaipur as the site, the official offered a hall to house the exhibit. Gus next sought out a sponsor acceptable to all factions. The choice was the Agricultural College whose principal, an alumnus of a Midwestern university, consented to deliver the inaugural address. Knocking on the door of every newspaper in town, Gus alerted editors and solicited their suggestions for servicing the press.

Two days before the opening date, a truck left Delhi, loaded with the exhibit, a moving picture projector, screen, pamphlets, posters, books, and other integrated materials. Aboard were Jack Maddux, Gus, and a projectionist to handle the films. Upon arrival in Udaipur, the group set out upon its various tasks. Sponsor, officials, editors, organization leaders were revisited and rehearsed. Newspapers were furnished abstracts of all speeches, in appropriate vernaculars. Engravings mounted on blocks—a service much appreciated by Indian editors—illustrated the texts. Posters went up in every section of the city. Jack met the press at tea, replied to questions, and ushered the group through a preview of the exhibit.

Several hundred of Udaipur's citizens attended the inaugural ceremonies to honor "The Common Man." Jack delivered the opening remarks:

Ambassador Mehta did much to build a bridge of understanding between your country and mine. We are here today to strengthen that bridge. When you study the photographs in this exhibit, you will see people wearing different clothes, living in different houses, eating different foods. Yet you will see yourselves in these pictures. You will see the same friendliness, the same love of family life, the same interest in work, the same desire for peace and freedom. You will realize the common man in India and America share the same cares and troubles, the same hopes and ideals. May this exhibit remind us of these truths. May they strengthen the human understanding that is mankind's greatest hope for peace.

The Principal of Rajasthan's Agricultural College replied. He thanked Jack for coming. His Rajasthani words echoed what I had once heard from a nurse in New Hampshire. "Ignorance is at the root of suspicion and fear. Thank God that nations are trying to reach each other with ideas and understanding instead of bayonets and bombs."

Reporting on the Udaipur experience, Jack wrote:

The six days of programming were filled with the usual varied, and somewhat exhausting round of engagements. I gave nine formal talks, plus several informal ones; drank endless gallons of tea (on one day I attended four separate teas); met with the press; inspected local institutions (everything from a rural institute to a lead mine); met with assorted individuals (from a man who claimed he has personal revelations from God to a group of graduate sociologists); was invited to private homes on three occasions; visited a Block Center and village; had breakfast with a group of Block Development Officers in training; discussed labor problems with union officials and management; met with the officers of a youth association; etc., etc. All in all, I had about thirty engagements; not much more could have been crowded into the schedule. There is no substitute for rubbing elbows with the Indian people. I hope they learned from me as much as I learned from them.

Over the year, the Americans of Delhi Post "rubbed elbows" with over six hundred thousand of the Indian people, some of whom had never seen an American before. They delivered over three hundred talks about the Common Man in America, in 49 cities. Their remarks were published by over four hundred newspapers in Hindi, Urdu, Punjabi, Rajasthani, Hindustani, and English, with a readership of twenty-two million. The cost was under $18,000.

In discomfort and disease the cost was higher. Amenities in the *mofussil* were almost nil. Hunger, heat, exhaustion took a heavy toll. Dysentery was chronic, and Maddux was hospitalized for weeks with hepatitis.

Nevertheless, the staff's morale ran high. It mounted in direct ratio to the difficulties encountered.

Difficulties were sometimes more amusing than hazardous—such as the day Maddux, rising to address a Town Council in Uttar Pradesh, was strafed by pigeons nesting in the rafters. Delivering a speech while dodging their droppings was the most arduous experience of his career. Tom Allen's nemesis was a question that pursued him from Agra to Amritsar. Whatever his theme, someone invariably rose to ask, "What is God?" Adept at fielding every other poser, Tom never evolved an answer convincing to the Hindu mind.

As for myself, my chief difficulties developed from my name. In Chandigarh, for example, the Speaker of the Punjab's House of Representatives, introducing me to a large audience in Le Corbusier's massive Court of Law, frankly voiced a widely felt suspicion.

"Two years ago," he said, "an American came here whose name was Loveman. Last year there arrived a man named Makepeace. Now we have Arthur Goodfriend.

Does America really believe we Indians are naïve enough to credit such crude propaganda?"

To what extent "The Common Man" improved the image of America in Indian minds was hard to say. Certainly success could not be measured by any count of column inches of press publicity. All I knew was that, in Sagar, the *pan* dealer's prejudices were clouded by doubt. And in a few hundred other villages, some fresh images of America were formed.

More important, perhaps, was that Delhi Post learned a little about Indian life.

We learned the meaning of Pandit Nehru's remark: "If the bond between a creative minority and the majority is broken, there is a loss of social unity in a society as a whole; ultimately that minority itself loses its creativeness and becomes barren and sterile, or else it gives place for another creative or vital force which society throws up."

We strove to strengthen the bond between the creative minority and the majority wherever we went. We learned to deal with elites in the context of the community in which they lived and worked. Tomorrow's elites were, today, anonymous members of the masses. India's problem was to close, rather than to widen, the gap that presently, and so dangerously, divided the elites and the masses.

We learned to respond to the people's self-interest. We brought our message as close as we could to the places where they lived. We sought to make Americans less strange, and more like themselves. We strove to identify America's common man with India's.

We learned that communication with the Indian people best occurred in the spirit of service. We learned the wisdom of give-and-take, augmenting their knowledge of America and eagerly accepting knowledge of them. We learned that the key to the most prejudiced Indian mind was humility.

We learned this about India's students: Americans could make no greater mistake than to be misled by their interest in our gadgets and culture, or by their admiration of our jazz. The sole standard by which Indian students judged America was what American experience had to offer India that, quickly and effectively, could move its masses into the modern world.

To workers we acknowledged that history's first mention of trade unionism occurred in India. Thousands of years ago, the Mahabharata had said, "The safeguard of guilds is union." Once unionism was established in a common context, Indian labor was eager to learn how and why the worker prospered in America.

We talked with farmers about American aid. We reminded them that every American crop, excepting perhaps tobacco and corn, had its origin in Central Asia. Presented in terms of reciprocity and exchange, American aid was fully revealed and gratefully acknowledged.

We talked about the dignity of man in communities where man had little dignity except in the realm of human hopes and dreams. We affirmed the state's subservience to the individual, and defined democracy. We quoted Lincoln: "No man is good enough to govern another man without that other man's consent." We quoted the Rig Veda: "In all that exists, and in all that could yet come, man is and would be supreme." We related democracy not only to the Magna Charta but to *samajnana*: "Meet together, talk together, let your minds apprehend alike."

We described the web of individual, corporate, and federal plans that determined the course of America's economy, and the regulations and controls by which individual incentives were balanced with the public interest. We revealed the folly of letting such labels as capitalism and socialism obstruct understanding. We told how the consumer, through freedom of choice, influenced the fate of the biggest corporation. And to those who criticized the corporation, we recalled "the Corporation of the Fifteen Hundred," the union of traders established in India almost a thousand years ago—"brave men," Indian legend proclaimed, "born to wander over many countries ever since the beginning of the Krita age, penetrating the regions of the six continents by land and water routes, and dealing in various articles such as horses, elephants, precious stones, perfumes and drugs, either wholesale or retail"—the earliest prototype of modern "big business."

Lawyers and legislators, we learned, were pleased that the rule of law flourished in America, much along the same lines laid down in India two thousand years ago. Teachers became curious about American education which carried on the traditions of Nelanda, an Indian university renowned throughout Asia when savages still roamed primeval Europe. Even those who reviled America's "imperialist allies" were softened by the reminder that Indians themselves had been the first to colonize other lands, establishing settlements far from home that endured for centuries.

We learned about communism in India. We heard it speak cynically, in the language of the common man, crying out against his misery, voicing his hopes, comparing his poverty with the wealth of the West. We heard it warn against capitalist corruption. We heard it exalt social justice, brotherly love, human equality and solidarity.

We learned—as hundreds of other USIS officers in other parts of the world had long ago discovered—that the best refutation of Communist lies was not anticommunism, but an assertion of the democratic alternative. We learned how deeply democracy dwelt within India's indigenous institutions. America's role was to recognize and to help these native forces to express themselves.

We learned that Communism fits the Indian character no better than it fits our own. We learned there was no impediment between India and America that could not be overcome by frank communication. We learned the basic integrity of the democratic position, in India as well as in America.

Such were the lessons we learned. To know the India of the common man. To see the world through his eyes. To pay respect to his past. To deal with the present in terms of his experience and understanding. To augment his pride in his own tradition, fusing our Western ideals with his deepest ethical insights. To harmonize our hopes with his, associating the common men and women of America with him in his struggle toward a better future.

XII. Pundits, pimps, and performers

Day after day, with mad dogs and Englishmen, Eadie went out in the midday sun. Actually, during Delhi's summer there was no sun, no visible orb, no single source of light and heat. Rather, the sun suffused the air, turning each particle into an ember that scorched the skin, withered the insides of the nostrils, and suffocated the lungs. In this inferno, Eadie searched for a house. Competition for space in the capital was keen. Moghul palaces and modernistic villas had one thing in common: a Himalayan price. Eadie was hard put to find an unpretentious three-bedroom home. Whenever she settled on something suitable, either it would fail to meet the Embassy's specifications for "representational housing"—a PAO was supposed to live in a manner proper to his station—or it would fall to a diplomat from Ghana or Outer Mongolia who didn't quibble about the landlord's awesome rent.

Eadie compromised on a flat above Ford Sessions' in Sundar Nagar, a residential neighborhood inhabited largely by lower echelons of the international set. Ford, who was in charge of American Embassy housing, had the garden, garage, and servants' quarters sewn up, and what was left wasn't much. There was a hex on the place—three American families had moved in and out in rapid succession. But when our things were laid out in the rooms, we felt a twinge of conscience at living so high in a land of mud-walled huts.

It wasn't long, however, before the twinges of conscience turned to outrage and anguish. Morning after morning our shower would run dry, stranding me with lather to the lashes. Eadie would send our bearer with a bucket which the gardener would fill, grudgingly diverting his hose from Ford's begonias. Nor was bath water the only hitch. The dark fluid oozing from our kitchen tap was cool but not potable, while the water flushing the toilet was pure and hot.

Hot was a dirty word in our household. Each evening I'd find Eadie and the children oven-baked in temperatures more intense than anywhere in the city. The heat seemed to be coming from some hidden source. One Sunday morning, a plume of smoke provided a clue. It led to the fuse box in the foyer where the electric wires, incandescent, were burning the surrounding plaster and paint.

I ran downstairs to report the matter to Ford. His flat was like a refrigerator. Stretched out beside one of his three air conditioners, each running full blast, Ford was sipping a gin and tonic. He said I looked warm. I pointed upstairs and said the walls were smoking.

Ford patted my shoulder soothingly. "Cool off," he said, "and don't you fret about a fire. There's an extinguisher in my bedroom you can borrow whenever you please."

Eadie and I had agreed, before leaving for India, to live as close as we could to India's middle class. Our idealism wilted like a starched shirt at one of Delhi's diplomatic dinners. Our sons, Bret and Arthur, came down with measles, dysentery, and trachoma. Bret, additionally, had hepatitis and Arthur almost died of gastroenteritis. Dengue fever put Eadie on the rack. Maintaining survival conditions even at our exalted level proved almost impossible. To live close to the people remained a lofty ideal. But in time, entering other American homes, we too eyed the size of the refrigerator, fingered the drapes, and counted the air conditioners. Our living standard was neither honestly our own nor genuinely Indian, but a hybrid affair that proved nothing but our own naïveté.

What finally broke our spirit was the jackals. A garbage bin at the end of the street lured the furtive beasts. Night after night, Eadie sat up in bed, terrified by their shrieks. One evening, there was a scratching at our door. Arthur and Bret opened it and found a gaunt gray puppy dog seeking sanctuary. They picked it up and fed it a can of tuna in the kitchen. Then they bathed it, dried it, and tucked it into their bed where Eadie discovered the snarling creature next morning. It was then that we cried uncle. "I'll die for my country," Eadie wept, "but please, no jackals!"

When we moved, it was to a ten-room manor four miles from the office in an area with the Quaker-sounding name of Friend's Colony. Our time of austerity over, we brooked no compromise with American standards, insisting on our quota of electrical appliances. Much of the modernity, however, was sheer façade. Electricity was of two types— regular and high power—and fixtures rarely fit either. Blowouts and blackouts were the rule.

Our water source was the Jumna River, the intake valves being located just below the sewage outlets, and the river itself sometimes moving out of its banks and carving new channels some distance from the pumps. The telephone was not altogether a convenience. It rang night and day with calls for Dr. Krishna Rao, a former tenant. Or it chattered endlessly, as though a monkey were on the line. Indeed, some monkeys loved to listen outside an open window for the ring. Then, sneaking into the house, they lifted the receiver and held long conversations with bewildered callers at the other end.

To our sybaritic American style, we added some Indian trimmings. Eadie solved the secret of hiring help, reading between the lines of their recommendations, and learning that "Abdul is an expert at boiling eggs" meant Abdul couldn't cook. Soon servants, like oriental rugs, were everywhere under foot. Joseph, the bearer, was a handsome young Madrasi loaded with energy, gold teeth, and a mastery of the mysteries of a dry martini. Kitty left to have a baby and was replaced by Stella. Stella became a second daughter, and her child Flavian the third son in our ménage. Ajit Lal, our long, lean *dhobi*, had learned to read and write, but couldn't support his family of eight except as a laundryman. Das, the driver, was unique—an Indian able to drive a car under sixty miles an hour. Kali the *mali* turned the front of our house into a botanical garden and the back into a bower of sweet corn, cauliflower, lettuce, and beans. The children called the part-time tailor "Naughty Buddha." Squatting in the shade of the verandah, controlling his Singer with his big toe, and smelling like a goat, he turned whole pages of the Sears catalogue into silk and cotton wearables. And there were the cooks—an endless procession of men all nicknamed Mamul, after the first. Each dazzled us with his prowess for a week. Then, somehow, meal after meal of boiled buffalo put an end to our appetites as well as to our illusions.

There was, finally, the sweeper, Kimcherand. All day he swept the staircase from the bottom up, littering the lower steps with the debris from the upper, and wondering why the job was never done. Eadie was about to fire him, not only for incompetence, but for insubordination. One cold night, when the other servants were all away, Eadie asked him to spend the night in the house. Kimcherand refused. It took a lot of digging to find out why. Kim had a wife and six children back in the servants' quarters, and only one blanket. If he slept in the house, either they or he would suffer from the cold. To learn the seamier side of India, one needed to go no farther than one's own back yard.

One day I counted the total of my dependents in the servants' quarters. It came to forty-six, with babies arriving at such a rate as to arouse suspicion in the minds of professed friends about the source of such fecundity. The canard that I was personally responsible gained ground when a woman appeared seeking any kind of work and asking no pay. When Eadie asked why, she said she was barren. "Everyone who works for sahib soon has a child," she said. "Please, memsahib, once I have mine, I'll go away."

In time, our lives settled into something resembling routine. Jill, our daughter, was packed off to a boarding school in Mussoorie, a station in the foothills of the Himalayas. Arthur registered at the Embassy's school for American dependents, where classes kept step with standards back home. Bret toddled off with Stella to an Indian kindergarten, where he created an international incident by refusing to be one of the three little pigs that went to market unless his friends, two Muslim boys, would be pigs too. Since no Muslim boy would ever dream of being a pig, the impasse was overcome by playing Three Bears. "Chotah Chiriah," Little Bear, was the only name to which Bret thereafter responded. Indeed, favoring Hindi over English, he soon talked principally in that tongue, and conversation between us practically ceased.

Eadie picked up the principles of protocol, and mastered what *News Circle* called "gush." For newcomers to the social circuit, this eminently readable magazine offered free translations of "the party line." If someone said, "Why don't you all just introduce yourselves," she meant "Who are these people?" "Why don't you come to lunch next Wednesday?" was a way of saying "I can stand it if you can." "May I call you after I check the date?" equaled "Give me time to think of a good dodge." "So sorry you missed our party" was a ruse for "Just remember that we are one up." "All settled in your new home?" implied "Perhaps you'll now pay back some of your social obligations."

We began paying back a large accumulation of social obligations. Some were intimate affairs for close Indian and American friends, while others were more or less official. These last entailed a good deal of expense. While liquor was cheap at the Embassy commissary, a case of Scotch scarcely moistened fifty guests. Part of the cost could be reclaimed by filing a form with the names of most non-Americans invited, and certifying that their presence was in the line of duty. This involved far more effort than some officers were able to expend. The financial burden was overlooked by visiting congressmen who, though they enjoyed these affairs, sometimes complained that Foreign Service officers were "living it up."

On one occasion Eadie was deputed to entertain a delegation of these dignitaries and their wives. She searched for some surprise that might add to the fun, and hit on the idea of having fortunes told by my friend, the swami, who haunted the arcade outside the office. On this particular day he wasn't there and I asked Sadiq to locate the best palm reader in Delhi. Sadiq nodded and sped off to round one up. That evening he assured Eadie that the man was waiting behind the house, ready to mingle with the guests whenever she signaled. The evening was going along well when the moment came to unveil the surprise. All eyes focused on the *dhoti*-clad figure emerging from the shadows. It was one of Delhi's most reputable *pan* dealers, bearing a tray of leaves, betel, lime, silver foil, and assorted spices. *Pan* was a party favor some of our guests will never forget—or forgive.

Theater and concerts flavored life in Delhi. Augmenting amateur offerings was a stream of professional performers flown out from the United States under the President's Special Fund, administered by the Department of State and the Agency. Many left an impression of excellence, entering areas of the Indian heart and mind from which politics and polemics were barred.

Nor were American efforts all inscribed on the lighter side of Delhi's ledger. Many wives of Mission officers labored silently in the slums, hospitals, orphanages, and sanitaria of the city. Squalor, disease, death—all the depressing aspects of Indian life with which their men-folk dealt in terms of statistics—the women knew by sound, sight, and smell. From the Silver Jubilee Tuberculosis Hospital came a moving testimonial to certain consequences of the humanitarian work performed by Tom's wife, Rubi Allen:

Some people holding corner meetings in the *bustees* tell us that Americans are not good people. Their country is out to enslave us with their gold. They are moneyed people, and no friends of the poor. But the nasty propaganda about the U.S.A. and its people evaporates before the practical welfare and devoted work of Mrs. Allen.

I had personal reasons to bless the work of these decent Americans. When my best friend in India was dying of tuberculosis, his life was saved by the intercession of Gini Blair, the Wheat Loan officer's wife. It was no important personage for whom she found money, medicine, and blood. It was for my driver, Sadiq.

On the whole, American women often showed a surer touch than their men in understanding India's inner meanings. It was on the litmus of their nervous systems, rather than on their husbands' minds, that India left both its somber and happy hues. Flocking to the Ford Foundation's excellent orientation course on India at Delhi University, they were grateful for every crumb of knowledge about the civilization in which they found themselves, and adept at putting it to practical use in their daily lives.

My own life, most days, began with the morning papers. All five of Delhi's English language dailies and the airmail edition of *The New York Times* greeted me at the breakfast table. On a random day local tidings included a story about a farmer in the village of Seempati Nadar who refused to dispose of the month-old remains of his four-year-old grandchild. His defense was that a divine voice had told him that the child would come back to life within forty-three days of its death.

Another item dealt with an issueless woman in Delhi

who confessed a kidnaping. "My husband threatened to remarry if I did not have a child." This drove her to simulate a birth and to produce the stolen infant as her own.

The Labor Ministry made news by sponsoring a special train for miners that took them across the country, acquainting them with life above the bowels of the earth, and instilling in them a sense of nationality. Nehru welcomed five hundred of these men to Delhi. Dhanga, one of the miners, was interviewed by the press. "I have seen more things than I ever believed existed," he said. "Much that I have seen I do not understand."

On the industrial front, the papers announced a scheme to step up national productivity by removing the tensions between employers and employees through *yoga* lessons. "The scheme envisions a substantial saving in sickness and medical benefits, since diseases of the digestive system which form an important block of ailments afflicting the working classes can be confidently cured through *yogasana*."

Laying down the Delhi papers, I'd pick up *The New York Times* and read random items to Joseph, the bearer. To him, life in America, as reflected in the news, was utterly antic. And yet, when we both reflected on the differences, they disappeared. Indians and Americans both believed in divine intercession. Both valued children. In both the urge to change was matched by reverence for tradition. Both peoples were awakening to a wider world than the one they had always known, and much that they saw they did not understand. Both found solutions to problems within their own cultures that seemed odd to others. Differences between the two peoples were visible but superficial. The similarities were invisible but profoundly human.

At the office, the day's work divided into two parts. One part was paper. The other was people. In an operation as complex and far flung as the Information Agency's, much of the paper work was essential. Budget matters, activity reports, personnel evaluation—these demanded days of deliberation. Major decisions depended upon their accuracy. Reading also consumed a great deal of time. Culturally as well as in current events, a USIS officer had to keep abreast of America. Each week brought a new avalanche of books, magazines, policy guidances, and background papers. Above all, there was the Agency's creative output itself. Like food and ammunition to front line troops, these were the lifeblood of our operation. A daily wireless file of about four thousand words, culled from domestic and international sources by the Agency's Press Section, reached us by radio. Films, broadcasts, prototypes of new publications, packets of materials on every conceivable subject—women, labor, science, education, music, art, medicine, industry, defense, foreign affairs— arrived by mail.

Some of the Agency's creative output impressed me as excellent, reflective of an enormous investment of intellectual energy, let alone dollars. But much of it seemed to be raw Americana, indiscriminately selected, overabundant, unconcerted, and to foreign audiences, unintelligible. Of the imaginativeness and depictive skill to which the President referred in charging the Agency with its mission there was hardly a trace. Instead of evidence submitted to the judgment of men of differing background and blood, here was the American ego, prejudging its case in the light of its own values, and directing the verdict. The task of adapting it to local needs and tastes was left to us on the spot. But between us and India rose this paper wall. One day I had a week's paper work stacked up on my office floor. The number of items totaled 682. It stood over eight feet tall.

Delegating the paper work among eight officers in Delhi Post simply spread the problem without solving it. Inevitably a species of Gresham's Law prevailed: the bad devalued the good. Useful materials were swept into file cabinets and trash baskets along with the dross. I shuddered at the shabby treatment given such costly effort. Never was so much produced by so few to the utter indifference of so many.

Indian mail took much of our attention. Many letters aimed at clearing up basic disagreements between our two peoples. These were usually easy to answer. Others were not. What is the status of call girls in the U.S.A.? Are love marriages better than arranged marriages? Is the White House so called as an emblem of white supremacy in America? Is it true that some Americans get up at midnight and grope for something to eat? What would be the population of the United States if you did not reduce it by shooting people, as American movies show?

Paper work was drudgery. People were fun. Our office was a crossroads for Indian friends returning our visits to the *mofussil,* and for American VIP's, Agency officials, speakers, exchangees, entertainers, and tourists. Among these we tithed more than a tenth of our time, usually to own profit and pleasure. Paul Robeson, fortunately, canceled his plans and was not among their number.

But another American Negro came to win India's affection. "I want to learn more about the philosophy of nonviolence," said Dr. Martin Luther King, "and to see how it can best be applied to solve the color problem in

America. Christ showed us the way and Mahatma Gandhi showed it could work." He talked of the tragedies and triumphs of his people; of the Negro's new sense of dignity; of the feeling that they were as American as anyone else, with as much to expect and as much to contribute; of the vast strides they were making, through Gandhian methods, toward their egalitarian goal.

Into Delhi, too, came a prosperous businessman risen from the poverty of New York's lower east side. Harry Plissner had become convinced that the best way to make America understood abroad was to spread abroad its periodicals. He had set to work collecting and shipping discarded magazines. Wherever people hungered for the printed word, he sent his packages. Harry was hardly different from the hundreds of American tourists pouring into Delhi. Almost all came with minds and hearts as open as their purses.

I listened one evening while another American coped with the questions of Indian students. Criticism focused on the coarseness of American taste. The American nodded. "Most Americans," he said, "pride themselves on being liberated from their bondage to aristocracies in matters of taste as well as in matters of politics. True, the upper classes may have better manners than the masses. But the principle of social equality is more important to Americans than good manners. There are no class tyrannies in American taste. America's culture is middle class. The middle classes have access to much the same goods as the wealthy. No one knows where this phenomenon will lead. All we know is that the process of social change in America is fluid enough to allow for the upward movement of popular taste from below, and the downward movement of critical taste standards from above."

I learned a lot about my job from that American. He was Max Lerner, author of *America as a Civilization*.

Mentally, I classified all Americans who passed through Delhi as pundits, pimps, and performers. Lerner was a pundit. Another visitor, a highly touted expert on American foreign policy, was a pimp. We took pains to arrange for him a full dress meeting of Delhi's Foreign Policy Association, an august group with little respect for America's position in international affairs. Over a hundred savants came to hear how an eminent American would explain America's use of its enormous power.

"Historically," the speaker declared, "the United States has never had a foreign policy. It has none today. Now, as in the past, we react to world events. We improvise policy on a day-to-day basis."

The audience could scarcely contain its joy. Here was corroboration, from a highly accredited source, of a deep-seated Indian suspicion. Having won his listeners, the speaker tried to turn their agreement to American advantage. But the damage was done. The Indian chairman happened to be a journalist who had risked his reputation defending in the public print the inner logic of the American position. He whispered to me: "Never again!"

I escorted the speaker to his hotel. He could not conceal his self-satisfaction. "Empathy!" he exclaimed. "The secret of getting along is empathy! It isn't often, I'll wager, that Americans hit it off so well with Indian audiences!"

I nodded. "Remind me," I said, "to send you the Order of Lenin."

The foreign policy specialist was not unique. Other Americans sold out their country for a round of applause. In order to gain a point they were quick to concede a slur. Some simply fawned or flattered. Others confused rather than cleared up the Indian mind on important issues. Two economists, traveling together, used India as a forum for their conflicting ideas, one Keynesian, the other Adam Smith. Another pair engaged in a personal feud. Delhi *wallahs* outside a centrally situated hotel were treated to the spectacle of an American jurist calling his colleague a dirty Jew, and refusing to sit with him in another seminar.

The performers, generally, were superb. Typical was a svelte folk singer named Marilyn Child. Marilyn worked with me in the Punjab. "*Sat siri akal,*" she'd greet the crowd, "God is immortal"—the blessing of the Sikhs. To everything she sang she gave some local meaning. "When the Saints Go Marching In," her opening number, she introduced as *Milkay Chello*—"let's all go along together!"

I teased her about her corny approach, calling it a trick calculated to get a rise from the crowd, and to warm them up for the show. Marilyn shook her head. "You can't reach into another human being without knowing a little about what's inside. It takes a little work to find out. Sometimes what's inside is so strange, you can't connect. Then you have to use a smile, a friendly gesture, a few familiar words to show you're trying and that you really care. The whole point is—*you've really got to care!*"

The Director of the Agency also came to Delhi. Late one afternoon George Allen sat in the Golf Links conference room while, one after another, USIS officers briefed him on the operation: problems resolved, successes achieved, opportunities unfulfilled because we lacked enough men or money. Only Big Dan Oleksiw, the new PAO from Bombay, confessed the insufficiency of our understanding of India, and the inadequacy of our actions. As for myself, no alternative seemed honest but to tell the Director that, viewed from Delhi Post's perspective, much of what the Agency produced was nonsense.

Golf Links rallied loyally to the Agency's defense. But the Director, musing over the matter, touched its very heart. "Odd," he said. "Officers from overseas are rotated back to Washington to staff the program. Why should such people put out nonsense?"

It was a big question, and Delhi's sun had long since set.

XIII. The cobra and the mongoose

Life in Delhi was rarely dull. There were earthquakes and Republic Day parades, replete with elephants and jet planes. Tea with village councils, and diplomatic seats at sessions of Parliament. An occasional evening with the Soviet Cultural Attaché who loved to come to our home, bearing a loaf of black bread or a tin of caviar in return for a few hours of Count Basie and a lesson in beatnik. He called his wife a "squaw," admired our "pad," and said he wanted to "dig" America before going there on his next assignment. He had similar knowledge of Hindi slang, gained in the course of a rigorous training program for foreign service that had begun in his secondary school and ended just short of the Diplomatic School in Moscow, a two-year course to which he aspired.

Beyond New Delhi stretched India's landscape. It was changing before our eyes. Eadie and I drove up to Bhakra Nangal and watched the waters of the Sutlej tumble over the world's greatest gravity dam. Rising 710 feet in the Punjab, it was destined to irrigate a million square miles of desert. Bhakra Nangal was but one of dozens of dams and other engineering projects transforming India. We reached them by the biggest railroad system in Asia. Or by Indian airlines flown by Indian pilots. Or via national highways—as good as any outside the United States and Western Europe. We passed, en route, industrial estates producing chemicals, synthetic rubber, cement, aluminum, machinery, textiles, steel—this last reaching 2.6 million tons in 1959 as compared to one million tons at the beginning of the decade. We visited national laboratories where Indian scientists sought ways of utilizing the infinity of their nation's resources. Visible, too, were universities, technological institutes, and training schools for teachers, midwives, village level workers. India was more than the Taj Mahal. India was also an atomic reactor in Trombay.

A highlight for every American was the opening of the new Embassy in the Diplomatic Enclave of New Delhi. Designed by Edward Stone, it was the first to be constructed under the terms of a directive paralleling the mandate of USIA. American buildings abroad, a commission of architects had decreed, must be in keeping with the cultural, architectural, and climatic conditions in which they were built. Mr. Stone had obeyed his orders. The elevated base of the structure, the surrounding grille, and the central courtyard bore much of the Taj Mahal's beauty. Mr. Stone publicly confessed that "the Indian idea of buildings designed around cloistered gardens and courtyards is one I have long cherished." The building was a monument to East-West harmony. Prime Minister Nehru bestowed on Stone's brainchild his only commendation of a new building in India. "I am enchanted," he said. "It blends the ancient and the modern." A peasant said, "This beautiful building shines like a star above our night."

Lewis Mumford, in *The New Yorker,* put the point even more aptly than Mr. Stone, Minister Nehru or the poetic peasant:

The problem in creating [an Embassy building] is not unlike the problem an American lecturer faces in addressing a foreign audience: of retaining his individuality and his national idiom without making any blatant assertion of his Americanism—being, in fact, a better representative of our many-faceted national tradition by showing his ability to find common ground with his hosts. The ambassador who has not the tact to do this should be kept at home; the embassy that cannot create a likable concept of our country has not fulfilled a main purpose.

USIS inherited the Ambassador's old premises on Barakhamba Road. Over one frantic week end, offices at Golf Links and Janpath were vacated, and Delhi Branch Post settled under the same roof with USIS-India. Our two organizations were now in better position to meet, to consider problems, and to concert operations. But the same old issues impeded agreement. What was our task—to overpower India with Americana, or to find common ground with our hosts? What should be our method— press agentry, seeking maximum mention of America on the basis of day to day news, or a long range strategy, concentrating our thin resources on a few areas of genuine urgency? At whom was USIS aiming—a minority of intellectuals or the Indian people?

To delineate the audience it wanted to reach, USIS-India drew a diagram. Indian society was represented as a pyramid. The pyramid was sliced sideways into roughly seventy layers in a descending order of importance. The Prime Minister stood at the pinnacle. Provincial coun-

cils formed the base. In between were legislators, educators, the judiciary, and other influential segments of the
ruling classes. Then these horizontal strata were sliced up
and down, minced into "present opinion-molders" and
"potential opinion-molders"; "doers"—people who directed
the conduct of affairs; and "influencers"—elements sufficiently organized or articulate to mold, indirectly, the
course of events. Other vertical slices were labeled
"Western-exposed" and "insulars," a distinction based on
whether an individual had or hadn't knowledge of the
Western World. Finally, there were "social protest groups,"
right, left, and center. The result was scores of subgroup-
ings, called "gate-keepers," which presumably controlled
the flow of ideas influencing Indian public opinion.

In the end, the exercise simply rationalized USIS-India's
original intention to deal exclusively with elites. Con-
strained by the paucity of its resources, it could not begin
to tailor its output to the parochial interests of so many
specialized groups. All the various strata so carefully separated were recombined into a single, homogenized, elite
audience at which its output was aimed.

The degree of USIS-India's addiction to the elite audience principle was long obscured by the argument of
limited resources. With a low ceiling on funds, priorities
were essential, and it made sense to start at the top. Then,
suddenly, millions of Wheat Loan rupees, owned by India
to the United States, were released for USIS-India's use.
A meeting was called to consider the opportunities opened
by this sudden windfall.

In releasing Wheat Loan rupees, Congress had laid
down certain restrictions which limited their use, in effect,
to publications. USIS-India was already distributing four

American periodicals: *The Reporter, The Embassy News-letter, The American Review,* a quarterly compendium of articles selected from contemporary American writing, and the *Labor Review,* a roundup of reprints from American labor magazines. Agency-edited publications supplemented this list. All were aimed at India's educated minority of less than one half of one per cent. We urgently needed at least one periodical edited for India's workers and farmers, to compete with communism's mass-oriented picture magazines. The decision, instead, was to issue yet another magazine "for the Indian intelligentsia."

The audience chart designed by USIS-India reminded me of the Washington Monument, with the pyramid at the top enlarged, and the pedestal eliminated. The importance of the capstone surmounting Indian society seemed self-evident. Equally evident, I thought, was the impossibility of reaching the summit without ascending the base. The way to India's leaders lay through their constituencies. And the constituencies lived largely in places like Sagar.

News came to villages like Sagar via many channels. While no shortwave receiver existed to bring in foreign broadcasts, the signal of All-India radio was clear. Located in the tea stall, the receiver was rarely silent. It brought to everyone within earshot a government-edited version of events. Radio, in effect, was as much a government monopoly in India as in any dictatorship. It was the one medium that sustained USIS-India's thesis: it could be influenced only from the top.

With literacy increasing, however, newspapers were becoming a major link in the local communications network. By Indian rule of thumb, each newspaper delivered in

Sagar had five readers. Word of mouth did the rest. Within twenty-four hours of a newspaper's arrival, almost every adult had some conception of its content.

The headman's house served as an information center. It contained newspapers for neo-literates, issued by India's Ministry of Community Development, packed with schemes from postal savings and life insurance to pig-raising and family planning. Picture magazines in Hindi and Urdu—*New China, Soviet Land, Soviet Union*—revealed the good life peasants enjoyed under communism. A poster, flashing portraits of Nehru, Bulganin, Ho Chi Minh, Mao Tse-tung, and Chou En Lai, advertised the five principles of peaceful coexistence. Another poster asked: "What is the difference between an official and a leader?" The answers: "An official orders people. A leader takes the people with him. An official uses force. A leader uses love. An official says I. A leader says we. An official orders—go! A leader says: let us come together."

Periodically, *melas* or country fairs set Sagar agog. The roads were jammed for miles with gaily painted bullock and camel carts carrying rural people in their holiday best. Hawkers offered toys, balloons, and bangles. Children spun round and round on *chakkars*, primitive carrousels, and *jhoolas*, the thousand-year-old fathers of the Ferris wheel. Jugglers competed with soothsayers and photographers. Farmers guffawed at their distorted reflections in curved mirrors, or peered into kinoscopes in penny arcades. Loudspeakers blared *basanti*, harvest songs. *Rishis* prayed. Families that had not met in months were tied in double knots, women in one, menfolk in the other, each enveloped in gossip.

The fair had its serious side, too. Bookstalls displayed

almanacs and government publications on dairying, co-operatives, the Five Year Plan, and other subjects. Block Development officials lectured, using a variety of visual aids to bring the country folk into the flow of national ambitions and events. Machinery was demonstrated, and salesmen urged passersby to try their new tools, seeds, and fertilizers. Credit facilities were advertised by both government and private banks, with usurers lurking near the tea shops, toddy houses, and latrines. In another section cattle awaited auction, watered by bright-eyed boys. Women exhibited handicrafts, textiles, and earthen crocks filled with herbs and chutneys. Camel saddles, bullock whips, cane stools, and braided mats drew Bedouin buyers from Jaiselmer. Great mounds of red chilies—more than India could possibly consume in a century of curries—spiced the dust.

I wandered amid the stalls, homesick for the country fairs of my New Hampshire home. Hillsboro, Hopkinton, Contoocook—their similarity to Sagar's *mela* was uncanny. I could scarcely believe my eyes at the sight of Indian youngsters eating *buddhikibal,* or "old spinster's hair," just like our spun sugar candy.

Here, as in America, food had a spiritual connotation, representing the fruits of a man's labor, for which thanksgiving was owed to God. Here, as in America, the family was the most sacred of human institutions, exalted above the state, and the hub around which agriculture revolved. Here too was friendship, the same spirit of comradeship, of sharing, of voluntary association in pursuit of common ends that characterized my own country. And here, as in America, people valued, above all else, their freedom.

Haranguing the lowliest untouchable were politicians

from the Congress, Socialist, Communist, and other parties. Before national elections, indeed, politics enveloped
the village. Commissioners, magistrates, legislators came
all the way from Udaipur and Jaipur to woo the local vote.
The mind reeled at the things these Big Men promised:
education for every child, free medical and hospital care,
wells, dams, and irrigation systems to end flooding and
drought, and electricity to set the village alight. The
Communists lacked such lofty vision. Instead, they dealt
with local problems, such as doing away with restrictions
on cutting faggots in the forest, a matter of urgency to
some twenty untouchable families who made a living
supplying Sagar with fuel. Nevertheless Congress Party
candidates invariably walked off with Sagar's vote. It
always would, until the Prime Minister passed away, and
with him the last link with Gandhi. Which way the
political winds would blow after Nehru, no one in Sagar
knew.

Old men puffed their *hukkas*, frowning at the strange
ways that swept Sagar. But to the younger people, ideas
unheard of ten years ago were commonplaces. Socialism,
land reform, five-year plans, village development, peaceful
coexistence with China and Russia—these took their place
with marriages, crops, sickness, and scandal as Sagar's
favorite subjects of conversation.

Behind its sleepy façade, in short, Sagar was in ferment.
The headman was still the number one man in town by
virtue of heredity, wealth, and his connections with powerful Congress Party officials. But unlike colonial times,
when feudal chiefs were given almost total power over a
district in return for military, administrative, or tax collection services, the social and political structure of the

village was broadly based. Heredity, caste, wealth still counted. But they were no longer the sole determinants of local decision. Now men with intelligence, eloquence, an appetite for influence, and a following of people were elbowing into circles of leadership, their importance deriving from their personal gifts and from the size and militance of the group they represented.

Today the headman could make no decision without consent of the Council. Councilmen were elected by secret suffrage of all adults. Every organized group in Sagar was represented. The heads of the various castes, the organizers of ritual, leaders of religious and occupational groups: these and others influenced Sagar's fortunes in every sphere.

The Council ruled Sagar, but public opinion ruled the Council. Who formed public opinion was hard to say. The old hierarchic system still governed family life, with respect accorded to age, to position in the scale of kinship, and to the supremacy of males. But more and more, younger men, behind a show of deference to the head of the family, were acting on their own, egged on by nagging wives with greater drive than their spouses. The father still headed the household, but actual management often rested with the mother. Grandfathers still lectured the young, but almost as often it was these old men who listened, open-mouthed, to what the children brought home from their teachers and textbooks. Brahmins still ruled on religion and law, and Marwaris were the last word on matters of money. But humble tradesmen subscribed to newspapers, and passed on political opinions with every purchase. In Sagar, perhaps, no merchant was more influential than the *pan-wallah*. Dealing in Sagar's most popular item and mixing each wad to the customer's taste, none was better placed than he to take the public pulse, to control the flow of news, and to color it with the same crimson that characterized his quid.

And yet, even the *pan-wallah* was overshadowed by the *Patwari* who recorded deeds to the land and whose power over this most precious of all possessions carried over into political matters. No man, not even the headman, dared take issue with him. But for that matter, neither did anyone dare contradict the barber. Every villager in Sagar knew the adage: "Even the king must bend his head, this way or that, as the barber orders." And every villager also knew that many an opinion was molded over a cup of *santara*, the powerful distillate of molasses sold by the local brewer. Never was Sagar's collective mind more open to a new idea than when the brewer eased it with drink.

On the other hand, a claim might also be made that the untouchables held the balance of power. The largest single organized group in the community, it accounted for almost a fifth of Sagar's votes. Actually, public opinion in Sagar seemed to be influenced by a composite of all these factors and forces. Sheer numbers were casting more and more weight on the scales, but a contrary emphasis was also being placed on quality.

Indeed, if one were forced to nominate the most persuasive opinion-molders in a farming community like Sagar, the answer might well be its half-dozen most progressive farmers. Life and death depended on knowledge of nature, and on more than one occasion, Sagar had been saved by their sagacity. They knew how to forecast frost, and that cloudy weather brought weeds, windblown from the Himalayas. When neighbors needed help in castrating a bull, or in treating a coughing camel, they turned to these men who had the knack of sifting modern veterinary science in the light of ancient lore. They were the farmers to whom the Rural Development officials turned to melt Sagar's suspicion of new ideas. It was in their fields that seeds, fertilizers, and pesticides were tested and demonstrated. Not that they were prey to any fanciful whim of an upstart from an agricultural college. On the contrary, these prudent men had resisted the Village Level Worker who urged the people to wall their fields to save water. Taught by experience, they argued that drainage, not storage, was the solution. Time had proved them right. Silent men, they lacked the political flair to be councilmen. They belonged to no groups. They could not read or write. No newcomer to Sagar would have suspected their importance. Yet not a householder in Sagar had failed, at one time or another, to seek their advice.

Society in Sagar was an organic whole. None of its elements existed in isolation from the others. All were part of the community complex, and objects of community pressure. Almost everyone was molding the opinion of somebody else. The order and degree of influence was difficult to determine. Youth did not live only in schools, but remained members of the joint family. The teacher was not simply an educator, but also a land owner. The headman, the councilmen, the Brahmins, the merchants, and the faggot-cutters each had their own individual interests, but all reacted to the requirements of the corporate group. All knew that only as a unit could Sagar survive, and survival was instinct in the village.

No insider would attempt to unravel the intricate interlacing of familial, occupational, personal, caste, and other relationships that produced village opinion. For outsiders

to predetermine "target groups" to whom specialized messages might be addressed, on the assumption that these
might influence public opinion, seemed a risky thesis. On
the contrary, to split off any stratum of society from the
others, to defer to elites, to appeal to parochial interests,
was to arouse the jealousies smoldering in the village, and
to invite the hostility of Sagar as a whole. Any contrived
or conspicuous association with a single grouping predetermined on the basis of presumptive influence was
almost certain, in a society so small and intimately organized, to be quickly noted and resented by the rest.

The secret of winning Sagar's ear, and of influencing its
attitudes, seemed to lie largely in understanding and responding to the self-interest of the corporate community.
A nuclear explosion half a world away, killing a hundred
thousand people, scarcely rippled across the tea stall
tables. But a local man bitten by a local snake set tongues
wagging for weeks.

Snakes were a problem in Sagar. Cobras were attracted
to the village by its rats and mice, and sometimes bit
people with fatal effect. Every year the snake-*wallah* who
toured the district would come to rid the village of their
threat. Enticing them with his magic, the *wallah* soon had
a basket full of writhing reptiles. Then the villagers gathered in a circle to watch the classic struggle between serpent and mongoose.

Out of the basket slithered the snake, stopping short
a dozen feet from the civet. The two creatures eyed each
other for several seconds. Then the mongoose feinted,
drew the cobra off guard, darted beneath the hood and
sank its teeth in the throat. The serpent thrashed the dust.
Blood and venom spurted. As though pitying the other's

agony, the mongoose drew back. The cobra uncoiled and advanced. Slyly the mongoose slipped past the trembling fangs, slashing through the scales that sheathed the vertebra, shaking the limp, black length until it was dead.

The murmur of satisfaction that swept the crowd revealed another side of Sagar. According to all Hindu teaching, the people should have sided with the serpent. The cobra was Adi-Sesha, supporter of the universe, the umbrella, shield, and vehicle of Vishnu the Preserver, to whom women prayed for the gift of a child. Everyone in Sagar was brought up to revere the snake as a sacred symbol of deity. But no one in Sagar had ever been bitten by a mongoose, while many had lost kin to a cobra. Sagar identified itself with the mongoose, among the most humble of mammals, and not with the cobra, the king of reptiles. Brahmins might mourn Adi-Sesha's death. But the deadlier the mongoose, the deeper was Sagar's secret satisfaction.

Thus it seemed that something more than public opinion mattered in Sagar. For lack of a better term, it might be called "visceral opinion." It wasn't just information, or accepted values, or dogma that colored people's reactions to events. People reacted not only with their heads, but with their hearts, their bowels, their inner beings. Right or wrong, reason or unreason didn't always decide things. What mattered was the side Sagar intuitively favored.

The factors involved in successful communication with Sagar added up to one thing: the need to identify with Sagar. A nation or people too strange and unlike the people of Sagar stood little chance, however reasonable their behavior, of winning Sagar's understanding. On the other hand, a nation or people attuned to Sagar's experience, its inner nature, its fears and hopes, could commit the crudest breaches of international conduct without alienating Sagar's sympathy or respect. A dictator banging his shoe on a table could count on Sagar's support if it shared the emotions that prompted his behavior. An elected representative of a civilized people, nobly expressing a sentiment remote from Sagar's self-interest, left the villagers cold.

To USIS-India, Sagar was an anthropological abstraction, distant from the practical problems with which it dealt. Delhi Post's visits to the villages were called "safaris." The suspicion gained ground that I was infatuated with populism, filled with some occult faith in the "folk," and given to the glorification of the common people, whom I credited with a nobility, wisdom, and power they did not possess. And always, there was the question: "Where is the payoff? Show us one practical use for all you've learned in Sagar!"

I couldn't point to any payoff. All I could do was to go back to *The Discovery of India* and to read again what Jawaharlal Nehru had written:

New forces arose that drove us to the masses in the villages, and for the first time, a new and different India rose up before the young intellectuals who had almost forgotten its existence, or attached little importance to it. It was a disturbing sight, not only for its dark misery and the magnitude of its problems, but because it upset some of our values and assumptions. So began for us the discovery of India as it was, and it produced both understanding and conflict within us. . . . It was this spirit of India I was after, not through idle curiosity, though I was curious enough, but because I felt that it might give me some key to the understanding of my country and people, some guidance to thought and action. Politics and elections were day-to-day affairs, when we grew excited over trumpery matters. But if we were going to build the house of India's future strong and secure and beautiful, we would have to dig deep for the foundations.

xiv. The divorce

It is hard to know the exact moment in the relationships within a family when differences overwhelm the bonds that hold it together, and when it faces dissolution. But early in the second year of our union, it became clear that the incompatibilities between USIS-India and myself were beyond bridging.

Paradoxically, it was at a time when our differences seemed about to converge that the incongruity of our positions became most apparent. Delhi Post's operation had attracted attention in India's three other consular districts. Dan Oleksiw, the Bombay PAO, mobilized his own organization for a similar effort. Integrating all media in support of a single message, USIS teams thrust beyond the seaport city where they long had been confined. Madras too toyed with the idea, and USIS-Calcutta began to range the hills and valleys of Bengal, Bihar, and Orissa.

Aware that the nature and direction of the USIS operation in India was shifting beneath its feet, USIS-India appointed a committee to reassess its position. Endorsing what it termed Delhi Post's "multimedia activities," the committee recommended that they constitute a major part and a central core of the all-India program. The committee also made a special point of validating the President's statement of our function. Indeed, so emphatic was its belief in the harmonization concept that it added a sentence of its own. "The purpose of USIS in India," it stressed, was "to portray those aspects of American life and experience and the democratic tradition that evoke a response consonant with the needs and aspirations of the Indian people."

USIS-India accepted its committee's report without amendment. The "multimedia" concept was authorized for all of India. With logic, the headquarters organization assumed responsibility for the selection of themes and the production of materials. A new theme, moreover, was urgently needed. "The Common Man" had completed its schedule, and invitations were arriving for return engagements in the forty-nine cities it had played. The announcement that the first USIS-India project was ready came just in time. I eagerly accepted an invitation to a preview.

About thirty panels were lined up in the workshop on Mathura Road. The headquarters hierarchy and I, forming a sort of walking jury, passed in review. The first panel reproducing a painting of Christ delivering the Sermon on the Mount. The caption expressed the exhibit's theme: "Man Shall Not Live by Bread Alone." The next panel stated: "Be free from care and trouble and turn thy mind to things which are spiritual." Illustrating this advice was a painting of Krishna.

Then four fictional characters were introduced in photographs and text to reveal "the nature of culture in a democracy." The first was Sally, a comely stenographer who lived in Denver, Colorado. Picture-captions described Sally's cultural life:

"Sally takes her three weeks' vacation with her mother!"

"Sally and her mother spend days in Aspen, high in the Rocky Mountains, where every summer a cultural festival is held . . ."

"Then they drive to Grand Canyon National Park . . ."

"Sally meditates before nature's solemn grandeur . . ."

"Sally goes on a tour with the Park naturalist . . ."

"Sally visits her college friend in Albuquerque . . ."

"Sally's friend is directing a play for the little theater . . ."

"Sally visits the famous William Rockhill Nelson Gallery of Art . . ."

The second personality was Fred, a shop steward in Detroit. Culture to Fred was watching "Richard III" on television, learning to paint in a museum art class, and pursuing a do-it-yourself hobby in a splendidly equipped workshop in the basement of his home.

The third personality contrived by USIS was Arthur, a student at Columbia University. "Arthur," the captions stated, "is a serious young man. Arthur is writing a Ph.D. thesis in Indian history. His library is large. His budget is small. The answer is paperbacks. Arthur loves the dance . . . Arthur loves music . . ."

The fourth character was called "Farmer Jeffrey." In the long winter evenings on his Ohio farm, Jeffrey read the latest book club selection, played classical music with a stringed quartet, listened to symphonic selections on the radio, or went to church to view slides of India. "Jeffrey raises wheat," the caption explained, "but lives NOT BY BREAD ALONE."

Concluding the walk-past, we stood in silence. Someone finally said he was pleased that the exhibit included pictures of Indian as well as of American culture. Having Arthur do his thesis in Indian history struck another nice "mutuality" note. The Country PAO objected to a photograph of a well-known Indian educator on personal grounds and suggested the substitution of another picture. After a few other remarks, mainly of a complimentary nature, or critical of some minor detail, the group turned to me.

I was speechless. I didn't recognize America in "Not by Bread Alone." Not a picture, not a line squared with USIS-India's self-declared purpose: "to portray those aspects of American life and experience and the democratic tradition that evoke a response consonant with the needs and aspirations of the Indian people."

In my mind's eye I saw India's people. I saw Ram Dhar, returning to Sagar, trying to tell the headman, the land recorder, the *pan wallah* about Sally, Arthur, Farmer Jeffrey, and Fred. I saw India's farmers and workers, approximately 1,500 of whom could feed and clothe their families on the sums expended by these four Americans in pursuit of their cultural bents. I saw weavers in Kanpur's cotton mills, turning from the power tools in Fred's workshop to the hammers and sickles on the city's walls. I saw Indian intellectuals searching the exhibit for something with relevance to India. I saw agitators denouncing America's indifference to the people's poverty, pleading not for things spiritual with which India was surfeited, but for bread alone. I saw India's Hindus and Muslims. How would they react to the image of Christ? I saw India's Christians. They would be quick to note that "Man does not live by bread alone" had been uttered by Jesus to the tempter during His fast of forty days and nights, and not in His Sermon on the Mount.

The Deputy PAO coughed with impatience. I suppressed the questions trembling on my tongue. Did this display sum up all that America had learned in the fourteen years since posters of spoon-fed babies had been set before the eyes of China's starvelings? Was this the true fruit of America's vaunted genius in communication? Were these the common ideals that, drawn from all we knew about India and ourselves, might hold our two democracies together amid the encircling storm? Was this America's message to a world in which three out of every four human beings went to sleep every night on empty bellies? Above all, was this truth? Could the thousands of Indians who had been to America turn to their countrymen and say, "This is the way it really is"?

USIS-India regarded "Not by Bread Alone" as a professional product. Much hard staff work, reflecting months of effort by its top-notch talents, had been invested in the project. More than a dozen elements, from pamphlets to films, had been amassed in the exhibit's support. It bore the Country PAO's approval. USIS-India's self-esteem was involved. But so was our integrity. So was our credibility. So were issues that seemed infinitely greater in the perspectives of America's declining prestige in Asia, Africa, and other rising regions in the world.

In the end, I voiced my misgivings. The ritual that followed was routine. With a few feelings bruised, a few panels corrected, "Man Lives Not by Bread Alone" went on the road. Watching the mobile units roll, I thought of Goethe's saying: "Nothing is more frightful than ignorance in action."

No great blow was dealt Indo-American relations by "Not by Bread Alone." A few thoughtful Indians were moved by the disparity between India's and America's condition. Some wondered aloud whether this was the time for Indians to be diverted from sacrifice and sweat by the evidence of other people's pleasures. Many were amused that Americans should advise Indians to turn their minds to things which are spiritual. A few expressed gratitude for a crumb of the bread by which Americans did not live alone. But most were silent, or polite, and the press play was satisfying. Indeed, USIS-India felt justified in signaling Washington that another cultural success had been scored.

The criteria by which USIS-India judged cultural success I never comprehended. True, the index of American cultural activity was high, and almost everything USIS staged in Delhi drew sizable crowds. That the sum of American talent we presented yielded some positive result seemed likely. Its very formlessness mirrored a free society and this, perhaps, was both the intent and the justification. Otherwise, in the arrivals and departures of speakers, artists, educators, and entertainers, and in the design and distribution of cultural publications and films, I failed to perceive much point. To amuse a few elites, to impress India's intelligentsia with our virtuosity, to fill a few scrapbooks with the plaudits of the press—these, by themselves, scarcely compensated the effort and expense involved. On the contrary, the very volume, variety, and glitter of our cultural wares sometimes seemed like the contents of a woman's handbag, picked up by an indiscriminate hand and flung down on a foreign shore, littering the landscape with evidence of the owner's eccentricity.

The Communist cultural offensive seemed more sensitively attuned to India's nature. India was a multilingual, multiracial, multicultured country in which each ethnic group feared for the future of its cultural tradition. Soviet cultural exports carefully cultivated the idea that, under communism, folk cultures had nothing to fear. Uzbeks, Ukrainians, Georgians, Azerbaijans danced, sang, and played in costumes not unlike Indian tribal raiment in color and cut. The exuberance, the animation, the lusty rhythms, leaps, and cries—all made clear that under communism the precious folk idiom of the past was being preserved while people built a better future. They identified Soviet folk-art with India's own in a common defense against Western "mongrelization."

Many American cultural exports unwittingly abetted the Soviet stratagem. The more popular our offerings were with India's youth, the more they inflamed the guardians of Indian culture. The more sophisticated our presentations, the less they had in common with India's own cultural character. The deficiency in the American cultural product derived from a single fact: its irrelevancy to Indian self-interest.

To infer total inadequacy in the American effort, however, would err as much as to assert total success. Norman Isaacs of the *Louisville Times,* Roy Matson of the *Wisconsin State Journal,* Russell Wiggins of the *Washington Post,* were among those who strove to understand India as much as to have India understand America. They lingered long enough in each community they visited to deal, at professional levels, with issues of common concern. And in the performing arts Joel Rosen showed how a keyboard could not only transport an audience, but bridge a cultural gulf. Rosen reasoned that music was not simply an end in itself, but a passport to a world of Indian intellectualism few foreigners were privileged to explore. To win an audience's applause with his artistry, to bow to its acclaim, and to catch the next train to another one-night stand made no sense to Joel. His work in Delhi began after the concert hall closed and his audience slumbered. Then, through the night, sitting on our living room floor, he, Ravi Shankar, Chatur Lal, Ali Akbar, and the cream of India's musical world "talked trade." Before the sun dawned, these Indians understood that America was music and art, books and ideas, and not all money, materialism, and crime.

Experiences like these urged reconsideration of our cultural approaches to Indo-American understanding: The formulation of some sensible plan. The setting of reasonable objectives. The evolution of a "cultural corps," as Rosen put it, recruited from the huge reservoir of American talent. The rearrangement of artists' schedules, enabling them to stay on in a community long enough to cement friendships and to lay a basis for long-term collaboration. Concentration on fewer performers, more performances outside the big cities, greater efficiency in fulfilling our impresario function. These were USIS-India's tasks. The headquarters group controlled the channels to Washington where our cultural activities originated. No changes could be made in the uneven and indecisive pattern of our programming without a decision in Delhi.

USIS-India preferred to let well enough alone. Operational pressures took precedence over self-examination and fresh perspectives. The opportunities implicit in cultural communication remained unevaluated and unexploited. Victor Borge came close to summing up my feeling in his celebrated remark on Soviet-American cultural exchange. "We get the Moiseyev ballet. They get Cuba."

Culture was the tortoise of the USIS operation. The hare was the press. Cultural officers, many of them former educators, concerned themselves with the long-range, aesthetic aspects of American experience. Information officers dealt with the daily news. USIS press responsibility in India was heavy. Neither of America's two great commercial news agencies was entrenched in India. The Indian government's Press Trust, Britain's Reuters, and the Agence France Presse had close to a clear field. Sometimes balanced, sometimes listing to port, their attitude toward American actions reflected the shifting interests of their respective governments. Except for the Associated Press, which had a tenuous arrangement with the *Times of India,* and columns by Walter Lippmann, Selig Harrison, and David Williams, USIS was almost the sole voice of the American viewpoint in India.

Statistically, USIS placements in the Indian press defied belief. Delhi Post alone, in an average month, racked up over 20,000 column inches of Americana. Added to the increments placed by the other three Branch Posts, the figures suggested a strong pro-American sentiment among India's editors. Riffling the pile of clippings on my desk, however, led to the same misgivings I felt about our cultural activities. Some of the press pickup had the clink of hardness. Full coverage of a major American speech, a first-class account of Communist colonialism in Hungary or Tibet, an analysis of the Cooper-Kennedy Resolution in the Senate—stories like these testified to the efficacy of a USIS handout. But the greater part of our placements had an aimless, artless quality. The captions on the clippings suggested their worth: "Chemical blanket saves water." "Birds in porcelain—delicate sculptures capture reality." "Cat dreams—appliqué hanging typical of textiles in U.S. craft show." "Shirley Temple returns to show business."

Like its cultural counterpart, our informational program could be rationalized as being representative of the slap-happy nature of a nation where anything could happen and invariably did. By American definition, too, a good press was one that caught the wonderful variety of life in a free society. It was precisely this kind of fare, moreover, for which Indian editors seemed to thirst. Hollywood gossip, science fiction, examples of American opulence—the more bizarre by Indian standards, the greater the demand. To fit such news into a propagandistic mold would be to lower American journalism to totalitarian levels.

Of all these arguments I was aware. But an analysis of the printed evidence suggested that the extravagant, the trifling, the esoteric and the absurd summed up America. Such claims as we had on an editor's precious space we pre-empted with our nonsense, consolidating many an adverse image of America in his readers' minds. The clippings deluging my desk reminded me of John Adams' letter to Abigail, his wife. "I must study politics and war that my sons may have the liberty to study mathematics, philosophy, geography, natural history and naval architecture, navigation, commerce and agriculture, in order to give their children a right to study painting, poetry, music, architecture, statuary, tapestry and porcelain." The year was 1780, when America's freedom was as precarious as India's today and when, like India's, our fate depended on the mobilization of our resources to meet the disabilities and distractions that threatened survival. Three generations, Adams foresaw, must pass before Americans could lend themselves to life's loftier preoccupations. USIS timing in India, it seemed to me, was off by sixty years.

The completion of my study of our press operation coincided with the date when Delhi Post's monthly activities report to USIS-India was due. Upon these reports the Agency in Washington drew in composing the semiannual *Reviews* of its operations. Each Post vied with the others, attesting to its own accomplishments, and fortifying its claims with statistics, anecdotes, excerpts from letters, editorials, and other scissorings of success. I had no appetite for first place in this competition. More useful, I thought, would be reporting that replaced self-satisfaction with self-examination. Reviewing our performance, I wrote:

The vast majority of the materials placed by USIS in the Indian press is either flaccid, or feckless, or so far removed from the problems and realities of Indian life as to impel wonderment about the morality of an agency that dispenses such stuff in a country where newsprint sells at $200 a ton. What are we after with our output—column inches with which to impress Congressman Rooney, or some sensible impact on Indian minds? In our search for evidence of effectiveness, how often do we simply find self-delusion? To what degree do we encourage an Indian editor in the belief that, having given USIS eight inches of play on "Bananas Have Nerves," he must in all fairness give eight inches to a Tass handout on U.S. imperialism? How do pieces on "The Problem Film in America," "Shirley Temple Re-weds" and "Aluminum Foil Spheres to be Launched into Space with the Next Vanguard Missile" impress Indian readers with America's passion for peace, its antipathy to colonialism, its sympathy with legitimate nationalist aspirations, its long record of support for self-determination, its generosity to every new nation struggling toward the threshold of economic growth? How is it possible, in an entire month, to avoid the placement of one single identifiable positive piece clearly contrived to dispel the Indian prejudice against the alleged crimes of American capitalism, racism, materialism, imperialism? To what degree, finally, may our successful intrusion in Indian news columns be considered a form of cultural imperialism—and of a debased culture at that?

USIS-India's reaction was prompt and predictable. It rejected the report, terming it "phoney," "full of hyperbole," and "proof of unwillingness to play on the team."

USIS-India's defensiveness had another side: a hunger for credit. When our forces left Lebanon, for example, the Speaker of India's House of the People, not previously known for his pro-Americanism, admitted to our Ambassador that American intercession after all may well have been in the interests of world peace. The Country PAO attributed the Speaker's admission to the fact that "he was a regular reader of the *American Embassy Newsletter*." My own view was that the action itself had probably altered the Speaker's opinion.

Such differences didn't endear me to the Country PAO. He seemed especially irked by my emphasis on "indigenously oriented programming." "What Goodfriend means by this," he once complained, "is that we should not fail to tell Indians that when Thomas Jefferson was sweating over the drafting of the Declaration of Independence his main source of inspiration was the *Vedas*, the *Upanishads*, and the *Mahabharata*." The Country PAO, in his indignation, stretched my meaning a little taut, but his complaint was a true measure of our conflicting philosophies. Without specifically stating the source of Jefferson's inspiration, the Country PAO seemed to infer that it was purely

American. My own view was based on Jefferson's admission that the Declaration of Independence neither aimed at "originality of principle or sentiments. . . . All its authority rests," he wrote, "on the harmonizing sentiments of the day, whether expressed in conversation, in letters, in printed essays, or in the elementary books of public right, as Aristotle, Cicero, Locke, Sidney, etc." The great Asian classics were not excluded from his sources. Indeed, to me, the greatness of the Declaration lay in its expression of the mind of mankind: "the accumulated political experience of people all over the world throughout recorded history." Its authority rested not alone on the harmonizing sentiments of the day, but on the heartbreaks and hopes of the ages. In the Country PAO's interpretation and my own lay two totally different approaches to human experience, to America's message, and to cross-cultural communication.

By such disagreements was the divorce portended. Beneath their outer guise, however, was an inner intangible. USIS-India resented criticism and suggestion coming from Delhi Post, not simply for themselves, but because they reversed the normal relationship between higher and lower organizations. It was in headquarters that philosophical and doctrinal soul-searching should have seethed; it was Delhi Post that should have been the target of USIS-India's questions.

Sooner or later, under the mounting stresses and strains, the Country PAO's patience seemed bound to snap. It did. But oddly, none of these open disagreements impelled USIS-India to end our association. The very beginning had foreshadowed the ignominious end. Concerned by the continuing weakness of our motion picture program, I queried USIS-India one day about what had been done with the film proposals I had submitted over a year earlier. I was told that "the answer was, and would be, nothing." The reason was that even if my contributions were "solid gold," I had made "a mistake in tactics in putting forth, after only a few weeks in the country, a comprehensive country plan."

I wrote USIS-India a note. Overlooking the fact that we had submitted a set of proposals, and not a "country plan," I said the USIS program was suffering from the conflict. I wanted very much to clear up our differences and get down to work together. I urged an early meeting.

USIS-India quickly replied: "The three men you want to work with are unanimous in feeling that 'your tactic' was a mistake which you had never admitted . . . if by some positive gesture you indicated you were ready to accept our way of operating, USIS-India was eager to stop all this writing and analysis of memoranda and spend the time more profitably in planning and action."

Before I could think of some positive gesture whereby USIS-India's way of operating and my own could be reconciled, the Country PAO ended the impasse. Delhi Post, he ordered, would be dissolved.

In personal terms, the divorce was welcome. The questions I had brought to India were largely answered. While I didn't know all the reasons for America's failure to put across to millions of peoples overseas its desires and real objectives, I had a few hints.

Before long, events furnished an additional clue. The Government of India was soon to stage the greatest international agricultural fair in history. Sixteen nations, including the Soviet Union and Communist China, would enter exhibits. The Government of the United States had decided to mount its most ambitious effort in Asia. Over three million dollars—many times more than the cost of the total annual USIS operation in India—was pledged for the construction of an exhibition beyond compare. Four agencies would cooperate in its creation: the Department of Agriculture, the Department of Commerce, the Atomic Energy Commission, and the U.S. Information Agency. To USIS-India fell the honor of devising the theme.

I attended the meeting at the Embassy where its ideas were unveiled. The slogan of America's exhibit was "The American Farmer Salutes the Farmers of India!" The motif was revealed in an artist's sketch: an American farmer standing at salute. To ensure big crowds, Hollywood would be represented by its comeliest stars. Over a hundred thousand dollars would be spent on calendars and advertisements in major newspapers.

USIS-India's plans for America's biggest effort in Asia, in sum, would fix the image of America as a militant, regimented, debauched nation where even agriculture involved salutes, servility, and the exploitation of sex.

Listening to USIS-India's plans unfold, I recalled the words of a Washington friend, warning me not to buck the bureaucracy.

"It will break your heart," my friend had said.

My heart was all right. But in my gut I felt the first stab of an incipient ulcer.

xv. Country Fair

Washington dispatched an inspector and a special emissary to deal with the differences between USIS-India and myself. Through their intercession, the decision to dissolve Delhi Post was reversed. Additionally, a telegram from the Agency requested that responsibility for the ideological content of the American exhibit in the forthcoming World Agricultural Fair be transferred to me. The prospects opened by this action were not intriguing. I was groggy from almost two years of infighting with the hierarchy; another round invited a knockout. USIS-India had the height, weight and—Washington's recent actions notwithstanding—the reach.

No time was left to argue the matter. The World Agricultural Fair was scheduled to open its doors just five months hence. As though the size of the undertaking itself were not enough to demand from each of us everything we had to give, another development added urgency. President Eisenhower planned to inaugurate the Fair. His presence made it especially important that something be substituted for USIS-India's "American farmer standing at salute."

Delhi Post rallied to the challenge our new assignment presented. Its approach was foreshadowed by a report on India's predicament in the field of food production recently published by the Government of India and the Ford Foundation. Based on an on-the-spot study by a team of American specialists, the report scored the seriousness of India's plight.

India is facing a crisis in food production for the rapidly increasing population. Food will have to be provded for 480 million people by 1966, an increase of 80 million people over the ensuing five years. If elementary wants, such as food and clothing, are not satisfied, other freedoms may be sacrificed for the promise of food enough. It is clear to us that food production increases at the rate required cannot be realized unless an all-out emergency programme is undertaken. India's village families—men, women and children—hold the key to increased food production. More food will be produced only as rapidly as the nation's farmers and their families understand and adopt improved practices.

The timing of the World Agricultural Fair, in short, was providential. The American exhibit had a job to do. What the American farmer knew about the uses of science and soil had to be communicated to the Indian farmer—and quickly. As though to dramatize India's danger—and America's obligation—Delhi itself had just had a foretaste of famine. For a three-week period, a shortage of sixty-two tons of wheat under Delhi's average daily consumption of 248 tons had precipitated a panic. Prices had skyrocketed and queues had formed outside "fair price" shops set up by the government. Not until imported grain had been released from government *godowns* had the peril been dispelled. In the eyes of women and children lining up outside the empty bins, I had seen something that even the Ford report had failed to tell.

The Ford report, however, left no doubt that "it lay within the capacity of India's people to mobilize to meet the great crisis before them. Startling increases in food production are possible if known improvements are adopted in effective combinations." India had the soil, climate, water, and other physical resources to produce sufficient food. It also had a long tradition in agriculture. Three thousand years before Christ the Indian farmer was cultivating wheat, barley, lentils, peas, and sesame. The Vedas were the first writings to mention rice, cotton, sugar, and corn. The Mahabharata had referred to agriculture as "the root of the world."

Indian agriculture had failed to maintain its early momentum. But the skill and tenacity that once had made the Indian farmer pre-eminent were not lost. To revive his pride and self-confidence, to enlist his interest in new techniques—these were our tasks.

Lessons learned on our "safaris" to the villages now paid off. We remembered the farmers' pride and self-respect. If Indians were to take American techniques, they would first want to feel that they had given something to America. The list of such gifts was long. India had given America the orange, the peach, the chicken. Lespedeza, soybeans, muskmelons, strawberries, cucumbers, castor beans, alfalfa, flax—all had either come from Central Asia or were strengthened by Indian strains. As for cattle, as long ago as 1849 a Nojori bull and a Gir cow were imported to America, forerunners of the Brahman breed that enriched our cattle industry today. By recognizing India's contribution to American agriculture, we re-placed charity, repugnant to self-respecting peoples, with the spirit of fair exchange.

Our "safaris" had taught us that centuries of suffering had made the Indian farmer suspicious of strangers bear-ing gifts. If he was cynical and stubborn, it was with good reason. His struggle with the soil was pitiless. High-sounding words, pretty pictures, big promises were pit-falls he had learned to avoid. It was easy for outsiders to catch his eye and ear with an exhibit or a movie. It was hard to get by his guard. His ability to smell out fraud was uncanny. Technicolor and stereophonic sound were fine for the upper classes. What the Indian farmer looked for was truth. If he believed you, you had a friend. If you earned his distrust, you were dead.

Both the USSR and Communist China were mounting exhibits in the Agricultural Fair. Before consolidating our plans, I flew to Moscow to explore the Economic Achieve-ment Exhibition permanently installed in the Soviet cap-ital. Listening to my guide explain the wonders of Com-munist agriculture, I could foresee what my opposite number in the Soviet pavilion would say to Indian audi-ences: "Starting from a base comparable to yours in India today, the USSR has achieved miracles. Under socialism, we have done it within a few decades. What we have done, you can do too, once you break the chains of capi-talist exploitation. Look at our Sputniks and Luniks. Look at our robot tractors—developed not by an engineer but by Ivan Logonov, a humble driver on a collective farm. Ours is an agriculture of and for the people—people like yourselves."

Little by little, our plan began to evolve. It must stress characteristics Indian and American farmers had in common, building on shared experiences and hopes. It must strengthen India's conviction that it possessed the human and natural resources to attain food sufficiency, industrialization, and broad-based prosperity. It must lay out, one by one, the steps by which such prosperity could be achieved. It must convince millions of men and women whose eyes were glued on Russia's and China's "forward leap" that more food could be produced in freedom than under a totalitarian whip. Everything in our exhibit—architecture, content, publications, films, press output—must be concerted to say: this is how India can achieve abundance in freedom.

To USIS-India's question about Sagar—"Where is the payoff?"—the three-million-dollar American exhibit supplied a substantial answer. Sagar's *mela* inspired the motif of the American exhibit. We called it *Amriki Mela*—American Country Fair. Among the most beloved of Indian and American rural institutions, the *mela* symbolized values precious to all who loved and worked the soil: food, family, and freedom. Common to free men and denied by dictatorships, "Food, Family, Freedom" became our theme.

Now the question was whether the *mela* motif would simply become a decorative device, like paper pasted on a wall, or the cement that held the exhibit together. The answer depended on one man more than any other. Minoru Yamasaki was the architect commissioned to design the American exhibit. He had visited Delhi briefly to inspect the site. Now, on a drawing board in his Detroit office, the American exhibit was taking form. Flying toward our first encounter, I wondered how the country fair concept accorded with the blueprints shaping up in Yamasaki's mind.

The great Nisei architect, slight and thoughtful, listened

as I explained the *mela* motif. Then he led me into his studio where a model of the exhibit was unveiled. Its succession of low buildings and lovely gardens eminently fitted the country fair concept. Already in place were the vast open air exhibition area, the milking parlor, the individual buildings in rustic settings. Swiftly Yamasaki added an entertainment area for the children, a booth for 4-H demonstrations, tents for handicrafts, preserves, and other products of the household arts. I had had little need to worry about harmonization. Yama showed me an envelope on which he had sketched the first vignette of the exhibit's most distinctive feature: thirteen Moghul domes like those dominating the skyline of Delhi.

I asked Yama how he had arrived at solutions so similar to those reached independently by Delhi Post. He said he had decided that the best service he could render the United States was to demonstrate the ability of Americans to assimilate the best from other cultures. "After all, that's the American story: races, religions, ideas from all over the world mingling and achieving unity in diversity."

"What I want the American exhibit to exude," Yama added, "is beauty, serenity, delight. Somehow these are expressed in the idea of human friendship. Let us add friendship to our theme." Then and there, the slogan of the exhibit became "Food, Family, Friendship, Freedom."

Washington approved the *mela* concept. Jim McCormick of the Department of Agriculture rounded up a variety of country fair features ranging from a merry-go-round to a flesh-and-blood Hopi handicrafter. The Atomic Energy Commission put together what promised to be a hit of the show: a pool reactor that produced isotopes capable of revolutionizing Indian agriculture. Bob Hickok, who represented the Agency in the international trade

fair field, upheld the idea in the endless round of meetings that often dilute imaginative undertakings. He did
not always win. Despite his pleas, the material symbols
with which Americans manage to replace their ideals in-
vaded the exhibition. The dispose-all, the automatic laun-
dry, the electric stove and other chrome and plastic irrele-
vancies—all were there.

During my American visit, I searched for a film that
specified the steps toward farm productivity in some context Indian farmers could comprehend. None existed, nor
did time and money permit the production of the movie
I had in mind. Necessity again proved the mother of in-
vention. Teleprompter, a New York corporation specializing in ingenious audio-visual devices, had evolved a
method of casting still pictures on a partitioned screen.
Up to five images could be shown simultaneously, or in
various combinations, with subject matter and speed ad-
justed to an audience's level of understanding.

We had just three weeks to put together a show. In
New York's City College we found a young Indian student named Asoka Gangadin who fitted perfectly the
part of an Indian farm-youth exchangee. He agreed to
accompany a photographer and myself to my New Hampshire town. The willingness of the American people to
serve the cause of international understanding was demonstrated by my Sutton neighbors.

None was an actor. The kitchens, the barns, the sweat,
the fields, the chicken houses, the manure were real. So
were the cooperative, the grange, the town hall, the
church, the school. It was rural America, simple, earthy,
unvarnished, and believable, as seen through the eyes of
an Indian boy. The climax came at the Sandwich, New

Hampshire, Fair where, amid the flamboyant foliage of the New England autumn, we captured in color film the American counterpart of the Sagar *mela*.

We called the production "Gopal Visits an American Farm." For the sound track, Henry Cowell composed a symphony of Indian and American country tunes. His "Mela Suite" was an inspired blend of *hori, basanti,* and Turkey-in-the-Straw.

Andrew Heiskell, the publisher of *Life,* opened the magazine's vast photographic file to the Fair. From hundreds of the world's finest photographs we selected those with most meaning to our Indian audience. These were blown up into large photo-murals, and set out under Yama's Moghul domes.

> O Mother Earth! Confer on us the benefit of all
> you produce.—Atharva Veda
>
> Give us this day our daily bread.—St. Matthew

Captions like these memorialized the legacy of two civilizations.

To spread the *Mela's* message among the millions of farmers who could never see the exhibit for themselves, we wrote a script for a film. Its main characters were my old Sagar friend, Ram Dhar, and his wife, Sukh Devi. At the *Amriki Mela* they studied the correct combinations of improved practices by which hybrid maize could be produced on their farm near Eklinggi. Each of the steps, from seed selection to modern systems of reaping, storing, and marketing the crop, was carefully explained. On the way back to Sagar, the couple stopped at an Indo-American experimental farm and saw how the *Mela's* lessons were applied to Indian soil. A hybrid maize called Illinois 1656 was demonstrated, which would double their normal yield.

Responsibility for producing the film lay with USIS-India. In passing them the script, we drew attention to its only virtue, credibility. The purpose was not to entertain, but to win the farmers' trust, inducing confidence in new techniques. Phony actors, dramatic yield increases, unrealistic details would arouse suspicion. Instead of advancing the time table of modern agriculture in India, exaggeration would set it back. Excellence, honesty, relevance were essential.

Excellence, honesty, relevance were also needed in the stories to be released to the press. USIS-India insisted on undertaking this function, establishing for the purpose a special press unit duplicating Delhi Post's. We asked USIS-India for a series of specially written pieces by distinguished Americans competent to discuss the social, technological, and political aspects of agriculture in an Asian frame of reference. Only by contributions of the highest quality could the hazards of pedestrian press-agentry be overcome.

A third means of broadening the impact of the *Mela* message was through mobile unit tours of India's towns and cities. We asked USIS-India to produce a miniature of the *Mela*, incorporating its major ideological and technical elements. To assist in the task of broadening our audience, and of perpetuating its usefulness beyond the life of the fair itself, we wrote and illustrated a handbook for educated Indians, and a cartoon book, based on the Gopal screen presentation, for the less literate.

American aid to India was a final point to which we

drew USIS-India's attention. It had a direct line to the
Technical Cooperation Mission, which managed our economic programs in India. Headquarters was in a better
position than Delhi Post to design a display that clarified
the nature and extent of American assistance to India in
meeting its agricultural goals.

Between the demands of the *Amriki Mela* and Delhi
District, my days and nights were full. The Agency sent
a man to assist me. He flew down directly from Moscow,
where he had helped set up America's exhibit in Sokolniki
Park. Jack Masey's bright mind harbored no trace of pre-
tense or compromise on principle. Respect for Indian
ability, sensitivity to the Indian mood, a disciplined professionalism gave everything he touched both meaning
and beauty.

Other Americans arrived to staff the *Amriki Mela.* A
County Agent fascinated Indian farmers with his knowledge of soil and seed. Four-H boys and girls mingled with
Indian teenagers; no one could match the ability of unaffected American youngsters to meet others on common
ground. Farm wives—despite a push-button kitchen—
battled the myth that American women led push-button
lives. Allen Eaton, the octogenarian authority on New
England and Southern handicrafts, charmed everyone,
from the Prime Minister down, with his specimens of
American cottage industry.

My own most vivid memory of the *Mela* would always
be a group of farmers from Indiana, Montana, Minnesota,
and Vermont who manned the machines and displays.
They listened to an Indian describe the ancient system
of *Nakshatras* or weather prediction. Reciting an ancient
quatrain, the Indian revealed that a cloudy day followed

by a clear night with a crimson moon was a sure sign of approaching dry weather. "Why sure," an American exclaimed, "like a red sky at night is a shepherd's delight!"

The plane flew in low from the sunset and circled the field. The gravity of a million welcoming hearts drew it down to earth. The President of the United States stepped out of the four-engined jet and entered the pageantry of the middle ages. Thousands of villagers hailed the "King of America" on the way from the airport. Delhi itself was aflame with flowers, but nowhere did the brilliance dazzle so much as in the Fair Grounds. In what a few weeks before had been a sea of mud stood almost a hundred buildings flying the flags of every Indian state and sixteen foreign nations. Above them all rose the *Amriki Mela,* its Moghul domes acquiring glory from the matching minarets of the Purana Quila, the ancient fortress in which they were framed. Yamasaki's pools reflected the beauty and excitement. To prime minister and peasant alike, here was an America all the more endearing for mirroring a little of India.

I dropped in for a last look at our exhibit before the President snipped the ribbon. A score of American farmers and housewives were busy readying their booths. Allen Eaton was humming amid his handicrafts. Yama was planting small trees beside the entrance. Jack Masey was at the rear, hoisting a placard into place. It contained a farewell to the guests, India's age-old greeting: "Prosperity to you of the good plow." In the background the music of Cowell's "Mela Suite" warmed the evening air. The pictures of Gopal flashed on the screen, reminding me of New England—of the Wells, the Bristols, the Kybergs, and of other beloved neighbors.

The chance to work with open, imaginative minds like these had renewed my confidence in my fellow Americans. Mutual understanding, respect, and cooperation were affirmed as the essence of the American idea. Eaton, Cowell, Masey, Yamasaki, and countless others had succeeded in giving the idea expression. They proved beyond doubt that America had not lost its human touch.

It was also clear that the exhibit was headed in one direction, while USIS-India pointed in another. The press coverage necessary to a wide understanding of the agricultural crisis portended by the Ford report, and the true meaning of *Amriki Mela,* was not provided. Instead, there was press agentry. None of the excellence, none of the byliners, none of the educational extension we hoped for was forthcoming. But the column inch count on "publicity" accurately indicated an insatiable appetite for recognition.

The four Branch Posts were supplied with a special farming exhibit to tour the countryside. Entitled "Agriculture in America," it boasted of America's advanced techniques and unparalleled abundance. Scrupulously avoided was any mention of the *Mela* motif and message: the applicability of American techniques to Indian agriculture.

The movie of Ram Dhar and his visit to the exhibit was not made. Money was insufficient for the production of a first-class film. It was spent instead on a quarter of a million calendars for India's "opinion molders." Thousands of dollars went into paper and print, but funds for postage were forgotten. In the end, the calendars were seized by souvenir collectors at the Fair, or passed out to visitors in USIS libraries.

The three-million-dollar *Mela,* nevertheless, was depicted in a remarkable movie. It featured a poor Indian farmer who plowed his arid field in spotless clothes, his feet in leather shoes. A brief visit to *Amrika Mela,* a few conversations with Block Development officials, and his sandy soil was transformed into an Eden. Neither technique nor sweat nor time was visibly involved in the process. Whether the cynicism of rural audiences was hardened or softened by the film might never be known. But the *Mela* film reflected a characteristic of many of our movies. Whatever it lacked in credibility, it made up in technicolor and stereophonic sound.

As for the fourth element entrusted to USIS-India, the evidence of American aid, it somehow managed to transmute a two-billion-dollar program into a few photographs of a chicken farm and a fertilizer factory.

USIS-India was completely candid in setting down its position: "Those of us in Delhi who are particularly concerned with the success of this show," it wrote, "agree fully that while the show must be made meaningful to the Indian audience, we need not waste any time in placing a false stress on alleged Indian contributions to American agriculture. We hope that it will not be vitiated by too much obvious pandering to alleged Indian sensitivities. . . . We are eager to get across the message in every conceivable way, of the abundance of American farms, the ability of the American farmer, his willingness to share, his spiritual heritage and the other aspects outlined in the show *in a completely American context.*"

The underlining was USIS-India's and not my own.

The President of the United States did not put the show in a completely American context. The words with which he opened the Fair were these:

Men, right now, possess the knowledge and the resources for a successful world-wide war against hunger—the sort of war that dignifies and exalts human beings. The exhibits here prove that.

The call to that genuinely noble war is enunciated in the theme of the American exhibit:

Food—Family—Friendship—Freedom.

Into these four words are compressed the daily needs, the high purposes, the deep feelings, the ageless aspirations that unite Indians and Americans under one banner—the banner of human dignity.

Here are four words that are mightier than arms and bombs; mightier than machines and money; mightier than any empire that ruled the past or threatens the future.

Here are four words that can lift the souls of men to a high plane of mutual effort, sustained effort, the most rewarding effort that can be proposed to mankind.

Food—that our bodies may be fit for every task and duty and service; our minds free from the fear of hunger; our eyes, undimmed by the tragedies of famine, searching out new horizons; our aspirations and our plans for their achievement not frustrated by failure of crop or catastrophe of weather.

Family—that in our homes there may be decent living and bright hope; children, no longer doomed to misery in peace and sudden death in war, their elders, no longer broken by want and sorrow beyond their control to mind or cure.

Friendship—that among all the peoples of earth the darkness of ignorance and fear and distrust will dissolve in the light of knowledge and understanding. The time has come when we must all live together for our mutual betterment or we shall all suffer harsh, possibly the final, penalty.

Freedom—that on all continents and islands of the earth every man and woman of good will and good life may make the proudest of human boasts: "I am free; slave to no tyranny imposed by other men, by the accident of birth, by the whims of circumstances."

Shortly after the *Amriki Mela* closed its doors, I was summoned to my last session with USIS-India. The Country PAO said my judgment was "abysmally bad." My disagreement with USIS-India's policies was termed "destructive." Declared "unfit for any service overseas that USIS would ever have to offer," I was dismissed.

In a somewhat different mood was my farewell to my staff. Indians and Americans, they had stuck to the principles on which we had earlier agreed. They had given literal interpretation to the Agency's Presidentially directed mission. They had proved that the mission could be fulfilled. Hard work, discomfort, illness had been their lot, but nowhere in India had morale been so high. To these splendid men and women it was not easy to say good-by.

XVI. "Come down on the dusty soil"

The camel in the stall beside my bed began to cough. A buffalo snuffled and sleep fell away. I stretched for a few minutes, feeling the ache steal back into my legs and feet. Then, groaning, I swung them to the dirt floor and groped toward the crescent moon framed in the doorway. The yard was a giant latrine in which men and women squatted beside the walls. Nearby a man, muffled in rags, tilted an earthen crock for me. I washed my face and hands in the freezing water and dried them on my shirt.

Across the square a fire silhouetted shrouded figures entering a long, low house. Inside about thirty people sat cross-legged, facing a wisp of a man who led them in prayer:

Hari, Hari, Hari—
God, You are the Lord Buddha, the Lord Brahma.
You are the One without beginning, ageless, never-ending.
You are Allah, Jehova, the Father of Jesus,
The Best among men.

You are the enlightened One.
Hari, Hari, Hari

The old man rose. With him we filed into the cold silence outside, stringing ourselves into a chain that began an ambling march into the night. Ahead stalked a guide, his hurricane lamp tracing a path that twisted through the desert. Behind him strode the shawl-swathed figure of Vinoba Bhave, *acharya* or saint, gentle revolutionary of love. This was Gandhi's successor, beginning another day of his endless quest for social justice, land reform, and peace.

At his left was Damodar Das, his secretary; at his right Mahadevi Thai, his nurse. In their wake stumbled as motley a company as any *guru* had ever gathered. A fakir, naked except for a pink toque garnished with a peacock feather of extraordinary length. An insane attorney, smitten with elephantiasis, dragging his swollen scrotum in the dust, muttering obscenities against the English. A woman, bent and agile as a witch, her nose and lips erased by leprosy, nothing showing in the aperture of her *sari* except one enormous eye. The Chief Magistrate of Rajasthan walked apart from the others. A white-capped figure, stout and stern, he was trailed by eleven members of the State's executive, legislative, and judicial bodies. A young Englishman, Richard Lannoy, the brilliant photographer and author of *India*, strode beside Violet, his lovely Goan wife. Other men and women were anonymous in the darkness. Bringing up the rear, a saffron-robed monk monotonously beat a drum.

Lost in the suffocating clouds of dust kicked up by the column was a lone American. Twenty-three years before,

Vinoba Bhave had said, "If I can ever be of service, come again." I had taken him at his word. My time in India was almost over. Before returning to America, I wanted Bhave's help in trying to understand the heart and mind of his people. Dropping behind every few furlongs to empty my shoes of sand, I cursed the impulse that had driven me into this madcap adventure. Whatever my days and nights with Vinoba might reveal of India's heart and mind seemed hardly worth such mortification of the flesh.

Paced by the lithe legs of the sixty-three-year-old leader, the procession pushed ahead. Herdsmen, sleep still clotting their eyes, mumbled prayers as we passed, or returned Vinoba's greeting: *Jai Jagat*—Victory to the World! We detoured to a barn where Bhave blessed the cattle. Night was fading when we left the building, reveal-ing distant hills like hags' breasts, wrinkled, long and flat, nippled here and there with Moghul watchtowers. And every few miles, like Asoke Raha's poem:

> The old woman village, wrapped in a quilt,
> Sleeps soundly in the straw smoke.
> She snores with her head tucked down.
> The roads are wooden with sleep. There is no sound.
> Trees sleep, standing on one leg.
> Jackals are quiet in the bushes.
> Dew drops softly.
> There is no scratching of mice or bats.
> On one side lies the crop-cut field.
> A baby vulture cries out in a banyan.
> Its mother stirs and slaps it with a wing.
> Alone in the mist of a winter night
> The one-eyed moon, holding a broken lantern,
> Turns its steps toward Adampur.

At sunrise we stopped. Vinoba faced the new day. *"Shanti, shanti, shanti,"* he prayed. "Peace, peace, peace." We repeated the words. Then, heads bowed, we stood in silence until the monk's drum resumed the cadence.

By eight o'clock of a glorious morning, we sighted Rastapal, our destination. People lined the roads, laying the dust with water and petals. A committee appeared: The Governor of Rajasthan himself, his ministers of Finance, Rural Development, and Public Health, the Chief of Police, a General of the Army, and the heads of Rajasthan's Congress, Socialist, and Communist parties. Rastapal's Councilmen fell into step beside us, and representatives of every civic and religious group swelled our ranks to almost regimental strength. Conch shells were blown, cymbals beaten, and a schoolmaster led a score of children in a staccato chant:

Ahimsa, satya, asteya . . .
Nonviolence, truth, honesty,
Chastity, nonpossession, labor,
Temperance, fearlessness, tolerance,
Independence, equality, avoidance of caste distinctions.

Two bamboo poles, topped by a crosspiece of leaves and flowers, marked the entrance to the village. Families from distant places, the creases in their faces filled with dust, thronged the streets. Youngsters plucked at my sleeve. *"Darshan,* sahib," they cried, "we ask your blessing." *"Shanti,"* I said, feeling like a fraudulent Pope.

Outside a schoolhouse by the village square we washed in melon rinds filled with water. Carpets stretched in the shade, and on these we sat while men ladled a puree of peas on dried leaf platters. Women poured buttermilk into little earthen bowls, and passed out millet cakes. We scooped up the food with our fingers, then broke the bowls, disposed of the shards in a ditch, and washed our mouths and hands. A few spinning wheels appeared, their murmur mingling with the snores of those who slept, and with the chatter of supplicants begging for Bhave's ear.

Within the building the old sage held court, his back to a bolster, his goatee and eyeglasses waggling as he talked. Vinoba Bhave had changed in the twenty-three years since our first encounter. A duodenal ulcer and malaria had eaten him away. The ninety pounds that remained were little more than skin, bones, and a pillow of white whiskers on which his beaked nose reposed. Only his legs recalled the young man I had met in Segaon. They had carried him thirty-four thousand miles since our meeting and seemed capable of doubling the figure if his body did not first collapse.

The *Padyatra* or long walk had begun in 1951. Communists were killing and burning in a violent campaign to redistribute land. In the village of Pochampalli, Bhave asked the people why they supported the Communist cause. Would not peaceful means be better? Might not landlords give land to the poor if only someone asked? Before the crowd could scoff, one landowner stood up and offered a hundred acres. At that moment *Bhoodan,* the land-gift movement, was born. Accepting the gift as one inspired by God, Bhave began a trek across India. "I am your son," he told landlords wherever he went. "If you have four sons, consider me your fifth. Give me my share of your land, one fifth."

In eight years, Vinoba collected eight million acres. Some Indians scoffed at his methods. But for every Indian who shrugged him off as a saintly crank, two venerated him as Gandhi's heir and India's hope. More than once the Prime Minister had walked beside Bhave, asking the *acharya's* advice. "Make India's villages the nation's first concern," Bhave replied, "and *then* draw up plans." In Gandhi's *Sarvodaya*—"For the Welfare of All"—Bhave placed his faith.

India's fate, Bhave believed, depended on the people's initiative. Government could not save the people. Only the people could save the nation and themselves. Nor could the people rely on handouts from others. Rupees would have to be wrung from their own poverty. "Give before you take" was Bhave's motto. Giving, in time, entailed more than land. Labor, money, intellect, life itself —for all these Vinoba asked, and all these the people gave. Even children set aside each day a spoonful of grain for *Sarvodaya Patrya*, the upkeep of a village social worker by the village itself, and not by the state. Someday, Bhave dreamed, these village workers would combine in a mighty *Shanti Sena*, a Peace Corps embattled against illiteracy, civic inertia, poverty, and disease.

It was not for Bhave's beliefs and dreams, however, that I was walking with him to the villages. It was, rather, to learn the secret of his ability to touch the people's minds and hearts. What magic had made the Rajah of Ranka deed away a hundred thousand acres of land? What had made those most money-loving of men, the Marwaris, absolve their debtors of their debts? What had led Jaya Prakesh Narayan, an odds-on choice for Nehru's job, to announce his *jiwandan*, the gift of his life, to the *Bhoodan* movement? Today Bhave's presence had brought this village of mud-walled hovels to life. Camels, jeeps, buses, bullock carts—and even a Rolls Royce with a Maharajah's crest—poured into the assembly area. The people's turbans and *saris* covered the amber earth with a carpet of a hundred colors. As the sun sloped toward the west, the square pulsed with suppressed tension.

At a quarter past four, an emaciated figure moved through the crowd, mounted the platform, and settled itself against a cotton cushion. Behind sat the Governor and Finance Minister of the State. Slowly the *acharya's* eyes roved the restless crowd. "Sit down," he said. "You Sita, you Lakshmi, and you, Hanuman over in that corner. All of you, cross your legs. Fold your hands and close your eyes. And now silence, please."

Bhave's voice broke the hush. He spoke of one man who had belonged to this village. "He left here to serve the rest of India where his memory is blessed. People everywhere have the right to ask why the village of his birth is not a *Gramdan,* in which all the people together own the land. To own, you first must give. In every home there must be an uplift vessel where early every day each of you prayerfully places something taken from your daily needs. Those who make this simple sacrifice prove they stand for peace. And peace is the road to progress."

"Some say"—despite the microphone, the old man's voice was almost inaudible—"science is the key to plenty. They are right. I look forward to the day when every spinning wheel will be run by electricity instead of human muscle. But a marriage of science and violence would mean the end of the world. And so you see, peace and progress depend on each of you—on what you think and what you do. Now, this minute, make a beginning. Sit neatly, legs crossed, back straight. Now meditate. Put hatred out of your heart. Think with love and compassion."

Day after day the message was much the same. Dubbing individuals with names from the Ramayana always drew a laugh. The appeal to local pride visibly flattered Vinoba's listeners. Sitting up straight and meditating— these were first steps every villager could take with ease; it was touching to see their eagerness to do so. In every village, people responded to the old man's words like puppets pulled by invisible strings. Still, the secret of Bhave's magnetism continued to elude me. Such banal stratagems hardly explained the adoration in people's eyes, nor the opening of their purses. It was Damodar Das who set the matter straight:

One can talk for days about the dignity of man and the worth of the individual. Few will understand. But every man, woman, and child in this village knows that Vinobaji has walked ten miles today on his own two feet through the darkness, despite sickness and age. Why? For no other reason than that he thought them worthy of the effort. Similarly, it is of little use to talk about the unity of India. But the least literate of peasants understands that if one old man can walk from Kerala to Kashmir, India is a nation and each of us is its child.

Vinoba's charisma rubbed off on me. Every evening someone would bring me a handful of dates, or a coconut, or a kerosene lamp. Soon I was the center of a crowd. Long after the cookfires were damped and Vinoba himself slept in the schoolhouse, people kept squatting on the fringes of the lamplight. Sometimes they listened. Sometimes they argued and laughed. Sometimes they talked, opening shutters on a world as strange to me as mine to them. Mostly they just sat, silently, with the same ineffable expression they lavished on Vinobaji, seeking something they could not describe, accepting something I could not give.

In time, from the silences as much as from the words, came understanding of India's people. All the clichés were true: their isolation from the modern world; the rigidity of their social structure; the excrescences that still mired their religion; the subsistence level of their economy; the stagnation of their inner-directed, tradition-hobbled, uneventful lives. A few did not recognize the name of Nehru. Some had no idea that America existed. Local issues preoccupied their thoughts. In one village, for example, every mind was focused on the matter of bangles. Traditionally, the number of bangles a woman wore symbolized status. Social workers, pointing to the fungus caused by the filth that collected beneath the baubles, urged women to wash their bodies instead of adorning them with metal and glass. The world could have been in flames for all these people cared. All that mattered at the moment was bangles.

"History-less," some sociologists called these people— but their awareness of the past was acute, however it might differ from the accepted patterns of educated men. To equate their illiteracy with ignorance was a serious error. Just as the blind developed an extra sense of perception, so did uneducated men seem to acquire a special sagacity.

Since independence, too, the horizons of the villagers had spread. Knowledge of their nationality was bringing with it alertness to the conflicts that rent the outside world. Communists among them fed the Marxist mystique that tipped the people's sympathies away from the West. Russia, they told the people, supported India's causes such as Goa and Kashmir. The Soviet Union prized their folk arts and was one with them in resisting cultural encroachment by the West. In communism the people had their only ally against colonialism. Recognizing that so long as Nehru wore Gandhi's mantle, communism's hopes must be postponed, the Kremlin's agents prepared the mind of the people for the day, however distant, when patience with the Congress Party's corruption would end, and the moment was ripe for Communist action.

Some Westerners saw in Bhave's collectivist ideas a Marxist taint. But Vinoba's views on communism were clear.

The difference between Gandhi and Marx is the difference between two men, one of whom breathes while the other does not. For the first you must cook a meal; for the second, you must light a funeral pyre.

We need to eradicate poverty in India. If this can be achieved by fair means, why use foul? A thirsty man, if he can get clean water, will not touch dirty water.

The government is like a bucket and the people are like a well. The bucket can take only a small quantity of water from the well . . . but nowadays a wrong idea has gained way— that the bucket holds more water than the well.

Wherever Bhave went, around him assembled politicians and intellectuals. Removed by education or position from the caldron of village life, some came to warm themselves for a day or two at the campfires Bhave kindled. Others came like jackals, to feed and fatten on Bhave's leavings.

One was a well-known figure risen to the highest rank of Congress politicians. Day after day, he sat beside Bhave, composing an economic treatise for presentation to the next convocation of his party. Evenings, he would read us what he had written, polishing and repolishing his prose. It was dialectical materialism, undiluted. I asked him why he did not write his paper in the comfort of his Delhi office. "Oh no," he said. "Then it would be no better than any other bureaucratic proposal. Writing it here, I can offer it as representing the will of the people."

Another hanger-on was a high-domed professor in a Bengal university who decried the predicament of India's educated classes. His hatred of the *status quo* knew no bounds. Cursing the corruption of Nehru's regime, he lamented the betrayal of the people. He begged Bhave's blessing on his cause.

"But how can I help you?" the *acharya* asked. The professor quickly answered: "A word from you, Vinobaji, and I can get a high position in the Education Commission."

Bhave smiled. "Today you are an intellectual—an educated man who is poor and who protests the evils of society. What you aspire to be is an elite whose snout is in the trough and who no longer can see society's evils. I cannot help you. India needs intellectuals more than elites."

Another of my companions was a Communist from Travancore, young, talkative, and filled with conceit. Trudging the cowpath to Khoori he urged me not to be a fool. "Don't wait until communism captures America. Get in on the ground floor! All the advantages lie with us. The peasants and workers blame their troubles on capitalism and colonialism. They see in Russia and China symbols of rapid industrialization. They contrast the ethnic equality of the Soviet Union with Western arrogance and discrimination. But the peasant and worker are powerless to mobilize their own frustrations. That is the task for men like you and me—to harness their hatred and despair to our purposes!"

I asked him why he had come all the way from Travancore to walk with Bhave. He shrugged. "I am a politician. Walking with Bhave will endear me to the voters. Communism, if necessary, will bathe India in blood. But only if we fail to win by votes."

Could communism win by votes? "How can we lose?" he replied. "Lenin said, 'National tensions are something to exploit, not something to solve.' Show me a country with more tensions than India! Regionalism, communalism, language, caste, culture, religion, sex—everything in India lies ready for us to exploit. Our task is simply to use these ready-made differences to pry the country apart. Bengali against Assamese. Marathi against Gujerati. Hindi against regional languages. Regional vernaculars against English. Intellectuals against bourgeoisie. Peasants against Marwaris. Brahmins against untouchables. Hindus against Muslims. Sikhs against Hindus. Always, we feed these tensions, waiting for the day when they tear the country to pieces. Then we step in to put it together, using the USSR and China as our model."

Then Indians would follow in the path of the Soviet Union and China? The Communist nodded. "What works there will work here. Collectivization of land by force. Communes for the peasants. Factories for the workers. A dictatorship of the proletariat with the Party at the top. An end to religion. An end to all opposition."

I told him I was grateful for his candor. He laughed. "I can afford to be candid. But what of you? Can you tell me how America expects to win in India? Can you specify America's program once you have won?"

"America," I said, "doesn't want to win in India. All

America wants is for *India* to win. And the only plan we have for India is India's own plan for itself. That is the difference between your beliefs and ours. I think our beliefs are better."

The Communist said, "If your beliefs are better, why are you not believed?"

I said that many of my countrymen were asking that very question.

I said good-by to Vinoba Bhave. He was spooning curds and honey into his mouth and some of it clung to his beard. He looked thinner than ever in the midday sun but his spirit remained robust. I was carrying two *chapattis* to see me through my trip and he asked how I liked these Indian pat-a-cakes. I said very much. "Well," he said, "they cannot be described as untouched by human hands." I asked how, in addition to the fourteen languages he spoke, he managed to master such Americanisms. He said he was still a great admirer of America. I invited him to come to the United States and offered him one fifth of my New Hampshire land. "No," he said. "I cannot afford to pay one fifth of your New Hampshire taxes."

It was almost time for the *acharya's* midday nap and I turned to more serious matters. "Vinobaji," I said, "you have only to knock on Nehru's door and he will grant you almost anything you wish. Why then do you walk from village to village?"

"Because the moment I stop walking from village to village, the Prime Minister's door will not answer to my knock. He opens it, not to me, but to the people."

"But the people are numbered in millions, and you are only one. Doesn't it make more sense for you to deal with the one man who holds the power of decision?"

"In a totalitarian state, one deals with the one man who holds the power of decision. In a democracy, one deals with the millions of people. That is the difference between a dictatorship and a democracy."

"Vinobaji, is it right and proper for outsiders like myself to come to India to tell the people about my country?"

"Gandhiji answered that question long ago. 'I do not want my house to be walled in on all sides and my windows to be stuffed,' he said. 'I want the cultures of all lands to be blown about my house as freely as possible.' I think your work is not only right; it is necessary. But do not come here simply to propagandize the Indian people. Come to see, to listen, and to love."

"One last question, Vinobaji. I am going home soon. Have you a message for the American people?"

Bhave thought for a few seconds. "Americans might read *Gitanjali* by Rabindranath Tagore. 'Leave this chanting and singing and telling of beads. Whom dost thou worship in this lonely dark corner of a temple with doors all shut? Open thine eyes and see thy God is not before thee! He is there where the tiller is tilling the hard ground and where the pathmaker is breaking stones. He is with them in sun and in shower, and His garment is covered with dust. Put off thy holy mantle and even like Him come down on the dusty soil!'

"That is my message to America," said the *acharya*. "Come down on the dusty soil."

Postscript

I reported back to Washington in September, 1960. A yellow slip in my mail box said that Abbott Washburn, the Deputy Director of the Information Agency, wanted to see me. I had first met him through his work with the Jackson Committee. Upon this Committee's recommendation, President Eisenhower had based his statement of the Agency's purpose. For Abbott Washburn's integrity as a public official, and for his unique sensitivity to overseas opinion, I had high regard. I regretted that as a result of the low efficiency rating I had been given in India, the impending meeting might be our last.

Standing six feet two, Abbott had the modesty of manner, the softness of speech that so often go with size. He talked about the Presidential election upon which the nation had just embarked. America's image abroad was developing into a lively issue. Democrats alleged our prestige was at an all-time low. Republicans avowed it had never been higher. Whichever party won, he said, the Information Agency would be serving under a new administration.

For the incoming President he wanted to have ready an appraisal of the Agency's global operation. He asked me to undertake this task.

The ways of bureaucracy, I reflected, surpassed all understanding. Delighted by the reprieve, I plunged into my new assignment. Ten weeks remained before Election Day. During that time I discussed the Agency's performance with the Director and his Deputy, with their chief lieutenants, and with officers fresh from service in every part of the world. From 140 interviews emerged the Agency's self-appraisal.

On the whole, replies reflected assurance that the Agency's work was important, that improvement was imperative, and that betterment could come not from a recitation of victories, but from an honest avowal of unresolved problems and opportunities still unmet.

Clearly, the Agency had overcome the havoc wrought by Senator McCarthy, an achievement only those could appreciate who knew how close he had come to obliterating the Agency along with America's reputation for fair play. Its ranks reformed, the Agency was grappling with seemingly insuperable problems almost everywhere in the world. The burden it bore beggared description. Everything that happened—from the White House to the smallest southern school—was grist in the Agency's mill. Simply to keep abreast of America, to say nothing of fitting so complex a society into other people's perspectives, was a task the mammoth size of which I had barely glimpsed in India.

The Agency's people, by and large, were intelligent and sincere. True, confusions persisted among them that had no place among professionals aspiring to career status. Nevertheless, they ill deserved the emotional antagonism to which they were subjected each time United States prestige took a downward dip. Occupying an exposed and vulnerable salient, they were sitting ducks for cynics who mocked "America's yearning to be liked," and for purists to whom any effort to interpret America was "propaganda," and therefore vile.

Virtually without allies among the public, the Agency's fortunes rested in the lap of Congress. Here, where the problems of intercultural communication called for constructive cooperation, the Agency encountered suspicion and truculence. Disgruntled by America's dwindling prestige, but confused about the cause and cure, some Congressmen vented their frustration by hacking away at the Agency's funds. Budget stringencies set in motion a new cycle of unsolvable situations that added immeasurably to the Agency's task. Not the least of these was the wear and tear on the Agency's high command. Dealing with rear actions on the Hill distracted the Director and his top talent from their front-line task of communication with audiences overseas.

In short, interviews with a broad cross section of Agency officers compelled deeper understanding of their difficulties, and enhanced respect for their efforts.

These same interviews also made clear that many of the issues evident in India divided the Agency as a whole, affecting communication with Latin Americans, Africans, and Europeans as well as Asians.

Months before, in New Delhi, the Director of the Agency had asked a question: "Officers from overseas are rotated back to Washington to staff the program. Why should such people put out nonsense?"

The Director's question contained its own answer. Officers responsible for USIS programs in individual coun-

tries overseas, returning to Washington, became responsible for USIS programs all over the world. By virtue of
rank, some were assigned to the highest policy-making and
operational positions: Assistant Directors for Europe, the
Middle East, Latin America, Central and Southeast Asia;
policy and planning officers; chiefs of media. These senior
officers also headed promotion panels, and established, in
countless other ways, the content, direction, tone and
tempo of the Agency's activities.

The officers with whom I talked, generally, belonged to
one of three schools. The first school believed in the
"trickle-down" theory of communication. These officers,
among them many of the Agency's ablest administrators,
earnestly believed that the soundest use the Agency could
make of its limited resources was to concentrate them on
the educated minority that held the power of decision in
other lands. They saw USIA as a machine whose purpose
was to distribute, through its world-wide pipelines, Agency-
prepared materials among foreigners capable of compre-
hending American pictures and prose. For the machine to
function, its human parts had to be conventional, inter-
changeable and obedient to bureaucratic standards and
demands. Few of these officers, holding down essential
jobs at home and abroad, had had the time to attend the
Agency's training sessions. Generally, they viewed the
Presidential statement of the Agency's purpose with scant
respect.

One highly placed executive ascribed this attitude to
three reasons: "First, the President's mandate contains no
philosophical or doctrinal concepts of value to the Agency,
and USIS officers are sufficiently irreverent to say so. Second, the mandate is so vague, generic, and equivocal as to
be susceptible to a wide variety of equally tenable inter-

pretations. Third, the mandate is not a mandate at all, but simply a statement encouraging in the most generalized terms possible an idealized aim."

The second school included some in the Agency's senior ranks but was mainly drawn from those at lower levels, many of whom had undergone Agency training in communication techniques. Communication, to them, was more than a dialogue between elites. They believed the American message could have little meaning to politicians, publishers, students, or anyone else in other lands unless it responded to the agonies and hopes of the masses. Beneath the illiteracy, poverty, and squalor of ancient civilizations they searched for the human experiences that would build bridges between ourselves and other peoples.

No officer better personified this group than Francis Corrigan, aged thirty-six, who was killed in a plane crash while trying to reach distant villages in Laos. What his widow, Flora Corrigan, wrote about Frank applied equally to a host of others in the Foreign Service:

I think Frank thought that the most important part of being a USIS officer was to get to know the people and have them know you and trust you. He felt in his position that much more was gained by going on as many field trips as possible into the more remote areas in Northern Laos, not only to talk with the officials, but to talk with the villagers and, as you might put it, the "common folk." I have seen him doing the work that normally would be assigned to a coolie when the coolie had something else to do, going out to a village at the last moment to show a movie when the projectionist became sick and then perhaps the next day getting all dressed up to attend some official ceremony. I feel he had the respect and affection of all of his staff in Luang Prabang, and a good percentage of the local population.

The third group differed from the two main schools, but for a variety of reasons. Some objected to raising any issues about Agency operations on the ground that such discussion "rocked the boat." "Let each Public Affairs Officer arrive at his own decision," summed up their view. Others literally had no view at all. They simply did an honest day's work for an honest day's pay, never questioning the purposes or consequences of their actions. And yet another segment of Agency employees brought to the field of international communication the habits and outlooks instilled in them by earlier occupations.

To some former newspaper men, for example, editorialization, cultural frills, integration of output behind predetermined themes—such shenanigans were unworthy of any self-respecting reporter. Strict adherence to a straightforward presentation of facts, they insisted, should be the alpha and omega of the Agency's operation.

Educators, on the other hand, urged the Agency to get out of the "news business" altogether on the grounds that news from official sources was suspect, and that the function could better be handled by existing commercial corporations. They agitated, instead, for long-range cultural programs escalated from the elementary school to the university, embracing all the sciences and arts, and enabling educated minorities in other lands to fit the news into the fuller framework of American civilization. Opponents of this position raised the question of a foreign government's willingness to have USIA meddle in its educational affairs. What American university, they asked, would turn to official information agencies of other governments in setting up courses and seminars in subjects relating to other cultures?

Struggling to put these dissimilar viewpoints into perspective, I searched elsewhere for guidance. It came, in part, from the ordeal America was undergoing in Asia, in Africa, in Latin America. Everywhere we faced insurgency situations where the battlefield was the bush, the paddy field, and the village, and where all the power America could muster was useless except as it applied to the peasantry on whose understanding and loyalty victory or defeat depended.

Guidance also came from the Presidential campaign, then rapidly reaching climax. With the rest of America, I watched the two candidates in action. Both were appealing directly to the people. Their faces and voices entered almost every living room in the land. Not content with television, they were whistle-stopping in all the fifty states. Both stood outside factory gates on chilly mornings, shaking the hands of humble workers. Both chatted with housewives, with the unemployed, with teenagers, with invalids. They stood in tossing cornfields and in teeming city streets, making themselves known to the masses.

Neither man could alter his principles, personality, color, or mode of speech to meet local tastes. But the substance of what they said reflected exquisite awareness of local pride and prejudice. Both candidates related their policies to sectional situations. Both intuitively understood that victory belonged to him with the greatest ability to harmonize his policies with community interests. Both groped for the key phrases that had greatest appeal to peoples' hearts and minds. Once found, these phrases were repeated, again and again.

The campaign made clear, at least to me, the American pattern of communication. Its keynote was inclusiveness. It involved the widest participation of the American people, the substitution of citizens' groups for restricted political machines, the quickening of popular emotions so that every citizen felt a personal stake in the issues, and in the victory of his chosen leader. It revealed that the decision-making process in America belonged, not to a small elite, but to the people. It seemed to me this pattern of communication, this decision-making process, held lessons for us in our efforts to communicate with other peoples.

I felt impelled, finally, to seek guidance from the outgoing President of the United States. Dwight Eisenhower reaffirmed his belief in his original statement of the Agency's purpose. Far from being an idealized aim, ingenuously arrived at, he said it had been enunciated after a considerable amount of study and discussion.

I believe it to be a fundamentally sound formulation of what we are trying to accomplish with the Government's official information facilities and personnel—namely (1) to create understanding abroad of our policies and objectives, (2) to show people overseas that these policies harmonize with their own legitimate aspirations, and (3) to counter hostile distortions of United States aims and objectives.

Our policies, of course, will by no means uniformly please the ears of all those reached by our information programs. Arguments will inevitably rage as to whether United States actions and policies do, indeed, advance the best interest of this or that country in specific situations, e.g., the Suez crisis. But this does not at all vitiate, in my judgment, the validity of Point 2 above.

In the crucible of a free society the American people through their elected leaders must, in their own enlightened self-interest, reach policies that are in harmony with world-wide ideals of peace, progress, and human freedom. Those policies cannot and will not be consistently perfect, but our batting average is high and our honest concern shines through: we covet no territory, we mean to enslave no man; we give generously of our substance in the great undertaking of our age to enlarge the area of human freedom and human fulfillment. In this sense, as Franklin and Lincoln particularly realized, America has a unique message for the masses, as well as for the elite, everywhere.

The next President of the United States, John F. Kennedy, endorsed the mandate. Under Edward R. Murrow, the new Director of USIA, its philosophical and doctrinal directives continue in force. Whether, and to what degree, they will be given effect by the new Administration remains to be seen.

To the new Administration I passed along the results of my study of the Agency's operations. Underlying its 130 pages of observations and conclusions were a dozen beliefs:

One, an open society of mortal men, America is and will remain imperfect. The image of America cannot be improved by demanding the moral regeneration of the American people. Human imperfection, moreover, is not unique to America.

Two, the American people cannot reasonably expect an organization of 4,000 public servants to create an image of America at odds with the way of life of 180 million citizens. Each citizen must know that his actions cannot be hidden from the world, and that no amount of propaganda can alter the impact of these actions overseas.

Three, America's image is largely formed by movies, television programs, books, and magazines produced and exported under private auspices. Telstar and other devices will increase direct communication between Americans and distant peoples. The techniques of cross-cultural communication need to be known and practiced—not solely by America's official Information Agency, but by every private citizen concerned with his country's twisted image.

Four, to win the hearts and minds of men, America must identify with the hunger of human beings to be free. Free to be themselves, true to their own traditions, and not dupes, slaves, or imitations of others. Free to fend off alien isms, our own as well as any other.

Five, to hint that success against communism is synonymous with American supremacy, is to negate the American case and to confuse our aims with communism's.

Six, America's prestige is not at issue. The issue is freedom's prestige—the commitment of other peoples to the democratic process in their own societies.

Seven, no one in the world will fight for America except Americans. Others will fight by our side only when the principles we espouse are self-evident in terms of their own experience and desire.

Eight, the only way America can influence the leadership elements in other lands is by understanding the predicament of the people, by relating American policies and actions to the amelioration of that predicament, and by communicating American concern for the common people in ways the people themselves, and not intellectuals alone, can understand.

Nine, men and women capable of interpreting America to other peoples are not produced by the ordinary processes of American life. Such persons must be trained. Senior executives of official agencies especially should be taught that success depends on understanding other civilizations as well as our own, and on harmonizing American ideals with the enduring aspirations of the human race.

Ten, harmonization is not a technique. It is a mood that modulates the mind and the heart, and an indispensable ingredient in intercourse among men and nations.

Eleven, Americans should not be ashamed of "wanting to be liked." America's glory is that its people *do* care, deeply, about the opinions men hold about their country. The depth of their caring, indeed, is the hallmark of their humanity, the measure of their morality, and the signature of their civilization.

Twelve, to restore the image of America is not really our task. The task is to hold up a mirror in which all men, everywhere, may see their own finest values, their own best hopes.

Acknowledgments

This book was begun on a Kashmiri holiday. It was rewritten on the S.S. "Sydney" en route from Bombay to Taormina, and on home leave in New Hampshire. Working evenings and week ends, the author finished it in Washington where, for a year, he was privileged to be a Federal Executive Fellow at the Brookings Institution, preparing a case study of Indo-American communication for the Information Agency's Training Division.

More persons in more places have helped him than the writer can possibly mention. To cite those who previewed the various drafts might seem, unfairly, to align them with the author's position. A few names, however, are associated with the long hours when the day's regular work was done and this purely personal labor was undertaken. In New Delhi, Rosemarie Birosak and Shirley Hayes, who over one steaming week end beat out the first draft. In Washington, Jeri Jacobson, who typed the second. In New Hampshire, Sheila Howe, Margaret Abbott, and Rita Hurd, who produced the final typescript. And everywhere, in every crisis, his wife, Edith Goodfriend.

To Theodore Repplier, special thanks are due for suggesting the title.

To the United States Information Agency is owed an obligation beyond the author's power to repay except in the hard currency of daring, dissent, and healthy controversy.

A.G.

ABOUT THE AUTHOR

Arthur Goodfriend is a foreign service reserve officer and specialist in international affairs. During World War II, he served with the U. S. Army in Europe and China and for a time edited *The Stars and Stripes*. From 1949 to 1957, he was Consultant to the Department of State, the Economic Cooperation Administration, and the United States Information Agency. At present he is in Africa for the USIA.

Mr. Goodfriend has lived for considerable periods in the Far East, Latin America, and Europe. He is the author of several government publications as well as eight previous books, including *The Only War We Seek, Rice Roots*, and *Stand Fast in Liberty*. Mr. Goodfriend is married and has three children.